CONTOU

FROM OLD TES
GW01425231

All royalties from the sale of this book
are to be given to:
THE SOCIETY OF MARY AND MARTHA
The Sheldon Centre
Dunsford
Exeter, EX6 7LE
(Caring for People in Ministry)

Contours of God:
From Old Testament Stories

by

ANTHONY HULBERT

Foreword by

MARTYN PERCY

The Canterbury Press
Norwich

© Anthony Hulbert 1995

First published 1995 by The Canterbury Press Norwich
(a publishing imprint of Hymns ancient & Modern Limited
a registered charity)
St Mary's Works, St Mary's Plain,
Norwich, Norfolk, NR3 3BH

*All rights reserved. No part of this publication which is copyright may
be reproduced, stored in a retrieval system, or transmitted, in any form
or by any means, electronic, mechanical, photocopying, recording, or
otherwise, without the prior permission of the publisher.*

Anthony Hulbert has asserted his right under the Copyright,
Designs and Patents Act, 1988, to be identified as
Author of this Work

British Library Cataloguing in Publication Data

A catalogue record for this book is available
from the British Library

ISBN 1–85311–105–8

*Typeset by Waveney Studios
Diss, Norfolk
Printed and bound in Great Britain by
Bell and Bain Ltd, Glasgow*

This book is dedicated
to all who have encouraged me
in the writing of it:
particularly: my wife Nicola,
my sister Victoria,
Rachel Stowe,
Liz Fossey,
Martyn Percy,
Margaret Ellison.

Foreword

> Earth's crammed with heaven,
> And every common bush alive with God;
> But only he who sees takes off his shoes.
> The rest are too busy picking blackberries.
> (From *Aurora Leigh*, Elizabeth Barrett Browning)

CHRISTIANITY is a religion of revelation. Yes, it is true that God is in some sense unknowable, a mystery that is unfathomable and can only be seen as though 'through a glass darkly'. Yet Christians have always affirmed that God can be known. In Christ, in the Bible, in love and creation, in suffering and joy, and in prayer, God is there. We do not reach God; God reaches us. Knowing and loving God often begins when we realise that God knows and loves us first, long before we were formed. Yet if this is true, why is it sometimes so difficult to know, love and experience God in the business of our daily lives? How can we be like Moses before the burning bush, and not like the blackberry pickers? How can we know the 'shape' of God in a world of distorted images?

The answer partly lies in the realm of discernment. We often do not see God at work because we look and listen in the wrong places; our eyes and ears need opening. Sometimes our expectations of God are flawed, in which case our vision of God needs challenging. But of one thing we can always be certain; when we begin our journey to find God, God's journey to us has already begun. Yet in that movement, and in moments of faith, there are risks. Sometimes our perceptions of God will be good; they will feel right, and the sense of a loving, immanent God will shine through. At other times our search can be a journey fraught with confusion and distortion, with God seemingly distant and unknowable. In getting to know God, and how God might know us, a good guide is always essential. So, Anthony Hulbert's book is both timely and welcome. It is a discerning book. Not only does he introduce us to the 'shape' of God, but he also roots his exploration in the diversities and apparent contradictions of the Old Testament. Chapter by chapter, we encounter an unfolding vision of a loving, compassionate God, engaged in dramatic and dynamic relationships with all kinds of individuals and peoples. It is a vision to be trusted, lived and shared.

Anthony's own spiritual journey weaves its way into his reflections. An Anglican Priest for over twenty-five years, he has been profoundly influenced by mystical writers such as Mother Julian of Norwich. His travels, his encounters with people and his considerable experience in parish ministry make this book what it is: deeply pastoral, profoundly spiritual, cunningly theological and, above all, faithful to his vision and experience of God. Anthony writes out of the supreme conviction that God is love, is radically for people, and can be encountered, known and loved in return. Equally, Anthony also knows that there are seldom simple answers to some of life's deepest quests. The Old Testament is packed full of stories that contain some of those answers, yet there are always plenty of loose ends that beg yet more questions. When it comes to God, scratching the surface of one mystery only reveals another one underneath. This then, is not a book that sews things up, but rather opens things up, giving the reader both appetite and confidence for the Christian journey ahead.

As you read this book you will find familiar Old Testament tales retold, but with new light shone upon them; vividness, surprise and personal insight abound. The story of the Call of Abraham challenges us to examine our own vocations. Jacob's dream reminds us that encounters with God can sometimes be painful, and always leave their mark: a wound of knowledge or a scar from love. Moses and the burning bush illustrate the cost of discipleship and the commitment to an uncertain future that is part of the Christian life. Solomon's dream reminds us that God equips people in service, just as Isaiah's dream reminds us that the equipment sometimes gets in the way of an honest relationship with God. The story of the sacrifice of Isaac – in many ways an appalling saga of abuse – is expounded in a delightfully playful, postmodern style that brings fresh insights. In all these stories and more besides, Canon Hulbert shows that it is God who loves us, calls us, provides for us and redeems us, echoing Mother Julian's affirmation that, because of his love, 'He may never leave us'.

I would not be writing this Foreword if I did not know Anthony well. In the years that I have known him and worked with him, I have been continually impressed by his vision for ministry, his integrity and honesty in personal struggles, his reflective nature and prayerfulness. More than this, his knowledge and love of God and people has been a source of inspiration. It did not surprise me to learn that he has assigned his royalties after all his hard work so that others might benefit; in this case, it is the Society of Martha and Mary and those they help who will gain. It is these qualities, amongst others, that pervade this remarkable book and make it what it is: a good, sound guide to the 'contours' of God in the Old Testament and for today. It needs to be read slowly and allowed to indwell, for there is much richness and distilled wisdom that will lead to fresh ways of looking at God, and new encounters. As you read it, I hope that your experience will be similar to mine: new 'shapes' and 'contours' of God emerging, horizons broadened, with heart and mind renewed.

Michaelmas 1994.

REVD DR MARTYN PERCY
Chaplain & Director of Studies
Christ's College, Cambridge.

Contents

CHRONOLOGY

This book has, as its chief objective, the aim of helping people into the Old Testament and its world of spirituality, so that insights from the stories may deepen faithfulness in Christian communities today. This chronology may assist this process:

B.C. (Approximate dates):

1750	The call of Abraham
1700	Jacob's journey
1290	The Israelite exodus from Egypt
1200-1020	Period of the Judges, and the Israelite settlement of Canaan
1020-1000	Reign of King Saul
1000-961	Reign of King David
961-922	Reign of King Solomon
922	Division of the kingdom between Judah in the South and Israel in the North
850	Elijah
742	Call of Isaiah of Jerusalem
722	Fall of the Northern Kingdom
627	Call of Jeremiah
621	King Josiah begins a period of Deuteronomic reform
609	Battle of Megiddo and death of King Josiah
597	First deportation of Judah to Babylon
587	The Fall of Jerusalem Ezekiel begins his prophecies
540	Second Isaiah
400?	The book of Job.

Introduction

What kind of God?
How can we know him?
What is he like?
What sort of contour or shape does he take?

To talk about God is to try to make some silhouette or pro-
file of his nature, character and substance, though to begin
the conversation is to begin with limitation. In the words of
Anthony de Mello's quotation in *The Song of the Bird*:
'Every statement about him, every answer to your questions,
is a distortion of the truth,' for 'God is the Unknown and the
Unknowable'.[1] The 14th century author of *The Cloud of
Unknowing* writes of the search for God in these terms:
'When you first begin you will find only darkness and, as it
were, a cloud of unknowing ... This cloud and this darkness,
no matter what you do, is between you and your God ... If
ever you shall feel him or see him – as far as it is possible here
below it must always be in this cloud and this darkness.'[2]

Nonetheless it is part of religious persuasion that there is
an access route to God which is not only worth discovering
because of the veracity of the revelation, but which, once discovered, will in itself lead to an individual change and transformation of a crucial kind. The search for personal growth
begins with the search for God. The finding of God, however partial the discovery, is not only the finding of oneself,
but the beginning of a relationship in which one's own life
and the world around becomes transformed. The Christian
life is above all a search for holiness and change. It is not
about Church allegiance.

So potentially complex is the search for God that all sorts
of blind alleys and weird cul-de-sacs may be part of the journey. The Christian claim that man is made in the image of
God can become dangerously transposed into God in the
image of man. So often in Christian history, and in Christian
teaching, has God been presented as an idol to suit the culture or aspirations of the society or community of the day.
An obvious example is the authoritarian, muscular, no-non-

1

sense, play the game, and wield the stick God who has emerged at certain stages of public school religion.

The Christian understanding of God is primarily rooted, of course, in the revelation of Jesus Christ and through the great doctrines that stem from the doctrine of the Incarnation. That revelation in itself owes much to the Old Testament roots from which the historical Jesus emerged. In the pages of the gospels it is clear that Jesus claimed for himself, and revealed in his life and behaviour, a very deep and all-encompassing relationship with the God whom he proclaimed as his Father. The events which led to his crucifixion began with the trial for blasphemy before the Sanhedrin. The blasphemy for which he was arraigned was the perception which he had taught about the nature of God, and the contour which, for Jesus, he formed.

Christians approach God through Jesus Christ and Christian perceptions of God are Trinitarian in shape and understanding. The Gospel which Christians proclaim is declared to be 'Good News', though because of the cloudy nature of so much human behaviour the goodness of the news may sometimes be hard to decipher. One crucial foundation plank in the platform of the Christian revelation must surely be the expectation that it is possible to encounter God, and that the encounter will have a contour and shape of its own.

An encounter with God, when it has happened, will almost certainly reveal a validity and sense of assurance that is overwhelming.

Every encounter tends to teach the participant something new about God. No encounter will in itself be a sufficient vision, and each one will be limited by that opaque veil which seems to dangle between the divine initiative and the poverty of human response, which St Paul describes in 1 Corinthians 13 v 12 as seeing in a mirror dimly. Each one is likely, however, through the eye of faith, to offer some new facet of that kaleidoscope of revelation which, like some incredible diamond, is always offering a new face, sharp and brilliant. Our capacity to receive that revelation can be blunted by mood and obstinacy or self-indulgence and a multitude of other blindnesses.

Many Christians and indeed visionaries from other religious persuasions, appear, so often, to trap themselves in the splendour of their own particular vision of the divine nature. Thrilled by the brilliance of one or another encounter, they can find, as the diamond of God's glory continues to revolve, that they have limited themselves in their own myopia or fundamentalist restriction.

The object of this book is to consider some of the encounters with God described for us in the Old Testament. It is designed to help those who would seek God to perceive something fresh of his nature. Such an enterprise is doomed to inevitable limitation. These 'Contours of God' are offered out of the poverty of one person's faith story. They are presented only as glimpses, tiny windows of hope.

The craft of so many of the Old Testament stories, of the poetry, of the prophecy, is the craft of the story-teller and the image-maker. The very abstractness of the divine nature calls us into a world of pictures and feelings, of experiences and visions. The teaching is exactingly diverse and wonderfully personal. To trace contours of God from the encounters recorded requires a will to enter into that world of image and outline, of personal experience, of mystery, and of mystical truth. Such a world is not always a familiar one for the late 20th century western world. Religious faith often needs freeing to enter it. Organised religion, as expressed in local communities, is not always very good at exploring new shapes out of its old roots.

Each biblical text which has been selected tells us of an encounter with God by a particular individual at a particular time and place. All our experiences will be coloured by the circumstances, psychological background and mood of our current situation. Some attempt is made to present the context and circumstances in each of these particular encounters. There is also an attempt to use the text in the light of our own human faith experience to map, however imperfectly, some of the contours of the shape of the living

God, who in his transcendence is distant, but who in his imminence is closer than hands and feet. As the 14th century mystic, Mother Julian of Norwich, whose writings have helped me much in an understanding of God, would put it: God's closeness is such that we are enwrapped and enfolded. 'I saw that He is to us everything that is good and comfortable for us. He is our clothing which for love enwraps us, holds us, and all encloses us because of His tender love, so that He may never leave us.' [3]

Chapter 1

The Beckoning God:

The Call of Abraham

(Genesis 12. 1–8)

THE HEART of Jewish faith experience is the reality of deliverance through the Exodus and an understanding of the way God has worked and works through the experience of history. The patriarchal stories in Genesis have to be seen in the light of that well-remembered experience of delivery, and in the light of the oral tradition which had handed them down to a point in time.

Roots are always important. Very often it happens that when people reach middle age they start to research their family roots. It begins to become interesting where people came from, how they were called by the name they bear, what struggles and difficulties their forbears endured, what pressures and moods were part of previous family experience and how they may have affected individual temperament.

In the corporate memory of the Jewish people, the story of the call of Abraham is the root of faith. Some time around the year 1750 BC, in the fertile crescent between the Tigris and the Euphrates, during the complex migrations, invasions and power vacuums of the development of early civilisation, fundamental and far-reaching decisions were taken by one family. A man called Terah had settled in the ancient city of Ur. In due course he and his family moved north-west to a settlement called Haran. From there, they moved south. They appear to have been pastoral, migratory people, squeezed out by the well-organised Ammonite settlers who took advantage of the collapse of the Sumerian civilisation. Perhaps they were something like some modern gypsies: tribal, close-knit, on the move, but well resourced.

The text tells us that Abram, as he was then known, is called by God to leave a potentially settled existence in the security of his father's house, and adventure forth into a new land, where he would be blessed, especially with numerous

5

descendants. We are told that he was seventy-five years old
when this summons came and that the call involved a large
extended family and many possessions in the shape of flocks
and herds.

In the national gallery in Budapest there is a painting by
the 19th century artist, Josef Molnar, of Abraham leaving his
camp. Hungarian artists of the period seem to have been
deeply overwhelmed by the experience of loss. Again and
again, their pictures portray a sense of ending; of good relationships; of good experiences, through death, through war,
through tempest, through an arranged marriage, through a
child beginning at school. In the Molnar picture, the face of
Abraham reveals the sense of pain and yet resolution as he
sets forth with camels, women, children and flocks.

The text gives us no clue as to how the encounter with God
leads to Abraham's formidable choice. We are informed only
that God told him and that the command appeared to be irre-
sistible. Part of the irresistibility seems to be the conviction
that such an act of severance and adventure and of casting
forth will lead to its own form of blessing and reward. Indeed
there are glimpses, even in the story of the call, of the cement-
ing of a covenant relationship. In such a dangerous and fool-
hardy enterprise, the assurance of God's providence was to
be essential. At Bethel, Abraham builds an altar and wor-
ships and intercedes. In chapter 15, Abraham is vouchsafed
a vision: 'Fear not, Abram, I am your shield; your reward
shall be very great.'[1]

The search for God must involve a spirit of adventure. An
encounter with God is likely to place a demand for some
form of change. The personal will to accept the pain and dis-
comfort and uncertainty of the change, sows seeds of its own
kind of unpredictable and unforeseen harvest and reward in
the fullness of time.

The stability and constancy of God's nature ensures a per-
manence and expectation about relationship. The dynamic of
God's activity teases forth a response that leads to adventure
and change. The story of the call of Abraham teaches us that
God is not distant and uninvolved in the future of our lives.

On the contrary, he puts before us the complexity of choices and encourages us to respond.

In his teaching, Jesus declared that anyone who cared for his own safety would be lost, and that those who would take risks for his sake and the Gospel would find a new security. In our human lives, risk-taking is often frightening and unattractive. We build our own routines. We settle with agreeable neighbours. We accustom ourselves to behaviour patterns and familiarity. We put down roots of either a bonding or an inert nature. All this puts an illusion of control and order into our lives which we know to be potentially risky and uncertain otherwise. Taking risks leads to loss of control and a range of unpredictable and uncertain possibilities.

In the search for God, the will to be open to risk and uncertainty is an essential ingredient to our response. For our search for him is really his search for us, and his search for us will usually come in the shape of some call for change. When Jesus encountered Andrew and Simon Peter in St Luke's gospel, the brothers' capacity to catch fish even in the Sea of Galilee appears to have collapsed, until the words: 'Put out into the deep and let down your nets for a catch'.[2]

Adventuring in the faith is like learning to ski. The mountain slope looks sheer and forbidding as the skier tops the crest and slides down the slope. For the novice, every instinct calls one to lean in and hug the illusory safety of the mountain slope, but the only way to ski is to lean out into the openness of the descent.

The nature of God's beckoning will be various and variable. Christian history is full of stories of heroic changes from a settled and secure life out into the uncertainty of the future; from Dr Albert Schweitzer's astonishing departure in 1913 from a position of considerable academic distinction to care for the suffering in the Lambaréné leper colony, to Charles de Foucauld's immersion in the solitude of the Sahara desert after an early life as a French cavalry officer and explorer in the late 19th century. For most of us, the call will be much less dramatic or far-reaching. It may be a call to leave a secure and safe community to pitch a tent in a strange land. It is more likely to require risk-taking with relationships, with reconciliations, with family agenda, with the person next door, with the wiser use of time, with the readiness to offer imperfect gifts for training and enabling. What is sure is that a faith community should never stay still. There is no abiding city. The individual is always being summoned into some new adventure of response and endeavour. The God who beckons will always be beckoning. What he asks of us will always have its own level of folly and apparent impossibility.

An old lady living in a block of flats had been greatly troubled by the inconsiderateness of her next-door neighbour, a young mother who had little support, and few mother-craft skills. By taking the risk of offering to baby-sit the fractious and bad-tempered child, an interdependent relationship of mutual support gradually grew. At an office, relationships were bad. Everyone was protecting their own boundary. There were fears of redundancy and everyone was looking over his or her own shoulder. One of the managers took the risk of cutting down his already truncated lunch hour to offer this sense of alienation in prayer. He stood in silence by the convenience counter of the local post office, for ten minutes each day, because it was the only place to go. Absorbed in a crowd, he could shut himself off and open the channels of healing to God.

It is a strange reality of religious persuasion, as expressed in the local Church community, that far from being adventurous and open minded; far from searching for the beckoning finger of God; the local Church surrounds itself so often with every form of liturgical and behavioural stability and continuity, as if shutting out on purpose that capacity for alert watching out for the beckoning call of God for adventure and movement and change.

No one will ever know how, in the mists of ancient time, Abraham heard and then responded to that insistent call of God's spirit which led him to make such a radical and uncertain journey. Perhaps it was looking up at the desert sky with its myriad of twinkling, lustrous, sparkling galaxies of stars and yearning for something beyond himself and for something wider than the comfortable realities of herding and feeding. In the encounter, however it came, he engaged with the living God who is always calling us into something new and dynamic which will be our life, and to resist that conservative anxiety to avoid change which will be our death. Change, however painful, is nearly always creative.

An elderly, retired clergyman, disabled by deafness, found himself in persistent demand for counsel, for the taking of services and for holiday duty. This was particularly true in a large town parish where a comparatively young but inert vicar was often away. One day, the old man asked the churchwarden for an explanation. 'I am sorry to have to say it, but our vicar has lost his pioneering spirit,' was the reply. One indelible shape of the living God is that call to pioneering, adventurous risk-taking discipleship which will tend to beckon us into something new every day.

The Very Revd David Edwards writes in a chapter in *The Divine Risk*: 'What a strange thing it is that we tend to regard the Christian religion as a fixed object, when in fact it is always changing! It is not like a statue in a museum, or a figure in a waxworks exhibition; look – it moves! Like the human body, it has to change in order to live and perhaps that is implied by calling the Church the Body of Christ. All these changes involve risks, but the biggest danger of all would be timid conservatism which in the end meant ceasing to be active, ceasing to be involved. In religion as in ordinary human experience, there is only one alternative to a life of change and risk: it is death.'[3]

In the beckoning finger of God, Abraham saw the call to life, even in his advanced years.

Formerly mounted on the tower of old St Thomas' Church in Old Portsmouth, and treasured in the newly extended cathedral, is an early 18th century gilded ship. Its inscription reads: 'Ships are not built to stay in harbour'.

'And Jesus said to Simon and Andrew: "Follow me and I will make you become fishers of men", and immediately they left their nets and followed him.'[4]

Chapter 2

The Accessible God:
The Story of Jacob's Dream
(Genesis 28. 10–22)

THE STORY of Jacob's dream at Bethel appears to be the story
of a personal struggle. It occurs when Jacob is travelling
north from the Canaanite region where Abraham, his grand-
father, and Isaac, his father, had settled. Ostensibly, the journey back to Haran is about a search for a wife at the home
of his uncle, Laban, in order to keep the tribe pure and to avoid
sexual contact with the local women which had been the
practice of his brother, and which had distressed his manipu-
lative mother. The reality is that Jacob was a man on the make
who would stop at nothing to further his own advantage.

Jacob is travelling north because, aided and encouraged by
his mother, Rebekah, he has cheated his twin brother Esau,
and his ageing father Isaac, of a fertility blessing. The rivalry
of the two boys has developed from the moment of birth,
when Jacob is born second, holding on to the heel of his
brother. Esau becomes a hunter and Jacob a herdsman.
Rebekah's favouritism of the younger boy encourages the
rivalry. It is exacerbated by Esau's choice of local wives.

The idea of the stolen blessing is Rebekah's, but Jacob
seems to have been quick to connive in the deceit. Once
given, the blessing cannot be revoked, and Jacob, the
younger son, runs away with a birthright which is not strictly
his own. As we can learn from the rest of the stories of Jacob,
the subterfuge is well within his character. Jacob is a man for
the main chance and nothing is beyond his capacity for trick-
ery. Later we shall find him cheating his future father-in-law
and uncle in a bizarre piece of animal husbandry to gain the
strong and speckled flocks for himself, and leaving Laban
with the weaker animals.[1] When Esau discovers the nature of
the trick played on him, he vows vengeance, and Jacob,
encouraged by his mother, sets off for an unknown future.
The priestly writer of the tale sees Jacob as, despite all, a

10

choice by God, in the patriarchal story of Israel's origins; and, for all his shortcomings and for all his character defects, he is presented as the follower of some kind of vocation, and as an instrumet of the call of God. God's capacity to use human frailty and character-weakness for his own creative purpose is a constant theme of biblical stories.

So Jacob's encounter with God comes upon him in the loneliness and isolation of his escape from his brother's wrath and unprotected by his mother's wily and doting over-care. He comes to a place known as a locus of spiritual importance and vitality and, in the evening of the day, he lies down to sleep, using one of the sacred stones as his pillow.

Psychologists say that it is in our dreams that our unconscious selves are revealed. In times of personal turbulence and disorder, dreams become a major part of our being. All sorts of wild and jumbled experiences, fantasies and visions flood in on us. With the help of those skilled in psychological perception, our dreams can tell us something of our inner selves, can teach us how to order our lives and interpret the forces at work in us. Jacob's dream is of a stairway with steps rising to God, and of messengers from God ascending and descending. The encounter is in sharp focus. God reveals himself as the God of the past and the future. God will use Jacob for good. Jacob will become a blessing. God will himself be involved in his life and will accompany him both in the actual journey upon which he is travelling and in the moral journey of his life.

There is to be a direct and personal relationship between Jacob and God. The stairway is a route for accessibility from the individual to the divine. God is not unknowable nor distant, but he has sought Jacob out in the loneliness and isolation of his journey and in the folly of his behaviour. The angels, or messengers, are like a ladder of accessibility, ascending and descending. There is constant movement between Jacob and God. God addresses Jacob directly. He is chosen. He is of value. He is to be used. He will be a cause of blessing.

In the turmoil of his sleep, Jacob, the trickster, is offered the chance to become Jacob the source of blessing. The shadow side of Jacob's character is overruled by the promise of grace and protection, of land, and of descendants.

Later, in chapter 30, verse 24, we come across Jacob, fleeing with his family from the possibility of Esau's vengeance, across the Jabbok river, and into a wrestling encounter with God. The story seems to tell of the two Jacobs struggling with each other to find a sense of validity for the real man as an instrument of God's glory in the conflict of his personal sense of failure. The experience of wrestling with God is a real part of the contour of the encounter. The jumbled nature of our own character often becomes divided and fragmented, as the potential in us struggles with our own awareness of failure and hidden motive.

In the Czech chateau at Slavkov, home once of the Kaunitz family, there is an 18th century picture which shows the story of Jacob wrestling with the angel. In the eye of the wrestler there seems to be a sense of overwhelming longing as he appears to search for what he hopes to find. It is representative of the longing in the hearts of so many searchers for that new sense of dependent acceptability between us and God, which is so hauntingly part of the human experience. In us lies the capacity for a total and all-consuming relationship with God. So often that capacity is blunted and thwarted by all that places itself in the way, by the muddle of our jumbled personalities and our loss of self-worth. In the Slavkov picture, there is an image in the face of Jacob, a longing, which might be characterised by C S Lewis' famous words, recited as his body was laid to rest: 'These things – the beauty, the memory of our own past – are good images of what we really desire: ... For they are not the thing itself; they are only the scent of a flower we have not found, the echo of a tune we have not heard, news from a country we have never visited'.[2]

After Jacob has wrestled with himself and seen it as a wrestle with God, the text tells us that Jacob went on his way limping, for the encounter had damaged his thigh. All our personal struggles carry their own price-tag and wound mark. If we encounter God as living and real, he will damage some of those defences and blindnesses, with which we seek to protect our self- interest and sense of accommodation with what is least attractive in our motivation and aspiration.

The limping Jacob who has striven with God, seen him face to face and yet found his life preserved, goes on to meet Esau and to be reconciled with his brother. It could be that the story of the 'wrestling' and the story of the 'ladder' are really part of the same psychological struggle in which Jacob comes to terms with the contour of a God whose will to use him, accept him and heal him, is a reality which he cannot escape.

When Jacob awakes from his dream at Bethel, he is driven to worship and to declare his faith. As is common in human experience, he perceives that he has been touched by God and that the encounter took place in a way which could only be verified in retrospect. 'Surely the Lord is in this place; and I did not know it'.[3]

A young couple searching for God through a request for confirmation training declared that the beginning for them of a search for God was when they had travelled together over rough terrain in Kenya to see a famed lake. As they crested a ridge in the ground, the whole lake was set out before them, alive with thousands of flamingoes. The experience was so breath-taking, and so all-encompassing, that on their way back they found themselves saying, in their own way: 'Surely the Lord was in this place and we did not know it'.

Often the nature of God's accessibility is hidden from us until we have passed by. Scenes of great physical beauty, acts of great courage, faithful love and devotion, personal self-sacrifice and dedication, often bring us to an encounter with the God whose contour reveals itself in moments of unexpected grandeur.

Jacob, waking from his dream, is drawn into a sense of giving worth and worship to the God who has found him in his disorder and isolation. Again and again, in his or her search for God, the believer will find that the search which has been made is in itself always too far-ranging and that the reality of God's accessibility is often to be found in the very place where we had lain down to sleep. 'How awesome is this place! This is none other than the house of God, and this is the gate of Heaven'.[4]

There is much about the experience of being human which makes us think that God, if he exists at all, must be very distant and remote from the feeble struggles and moral failures of our ordinary lives. The Christian Gospel asserts of course as loud as it can be heard, that God has come close in the birth, life and death of Jesus Christ, our Lord. The contour of God expressed in the story of Jacob's dream is another version, in another time, in another place and in another culture, of the story of the Bethlehem stable, so movingly and graphically etched by St Luke: Emmanuel: God with us: a ladder between heaven and earth; God nearer than hands and feet. As Sarah Adams, the hymn writer, puts it in her Victorian poetry:

> 'Though, like the wanderer,
> The sun gone down,
> Darkness be over me,
> My rest a stone;
> Yet in my dreams I'd be
> Nearer, my God to thee,
> Nearer to thee!'[5]

And Jesus said: 'The Kingdom of God is not coming with signs to be observed; nor will they say, "Lo, here it is!" or "There!" for behold, the kingdom of God is in the midst of you'.6

Chapter 3

The God who Calls by Name:

Moses and the burning bush
(Exodus 3. 1–14)

MOSES' encounter with God on the mountain, called both Horeb and Sinai, is a profound event in the story of Israelite faith. The background of patriarchal journeying and wandering has been painted in. The promise of land and descendants and blessing has been prescribed. Following the famine which led the people down to Egypt, through the story of Joseph and his brothers, the Jewish people face oppression through the policies of Remesis II, who seeks to use the nomadic peoples as a source for cheap labour in his building programme.

The book of Exodus opens with dire predictions of sorrow and suffering for the Hebrew people. The stage is set for a trial of strength between the forces of wickedness as perceived in the policies of Pharaoh and the faithfulness of God in his fulfilment of his promise to the people he has claimed for his own. In the great historical drama that is to unfold, culminating in the exodus from Egypt, the appearance of Moses as leader and agent of God's purpose is crucial. Moses, whose birth and early salvation are, in Shakespearian fashion, coloured round with dramatic and miraculous supporting events to make him of immediate interest to the reader, emerges as a leader with a conscience and a destiny.

The setting of Moses' encounter with God is the loneliness and isolation of the desert. Moses has fled here, in fear of his life, having challenged and killed an Egyptian cruelly attacking a fellow countryman. Loyalties are uncertain and there is evidence that he might be turned in by a covert witness.

In the desert area, he befriends some women herdspeople, harassed by local marauders, and settles down with one of the girls, given in marriage by her father Ruel or Jethro, a

15

member of a local Midianite tribe. This man appears to have had a faith of his own, with a particular spiritual vision. While herding his father-in-law's flocks God appears to Moses in what is described as a burning bush. Moses is reported as saying: 'I will turn aside and see this great sight, why the bush is not burnt'.[1]

It is one of the vital requirements in the pattern of the contours of God that there be a capacity to turn aside and see. So much in our lives conspires against this ready reaction. No one will know what triggered Moses into looking and seeing and turning aside.

The text tells us that Moses is far from his own home and his people in Egypt. He has settled in a strange land. In the background there lies an anxiety about the possibility of being apprehended for murder. He is alone in the vastness of the desert, in charge of someone else's flocks, and he is already concerned about injustice and oppression.

Our spiritual vision is dependent often on a will and capacity to turn aside, and to see something of God in the disclosure all around us in the natural world. It is possible that the bush was a blaze of desert flowers, that it was so isolated in its shape and texture and position that it compelled the eye to look upon it. The fire is an Old Testament shorthand for the presence of God.

Most of us will never know what it is that makes us turn aside and see the great sight that leads us to God. A red admiral butterfly fluttering its wings gently in the summer sunshine; a duck disappearing into the grey, dappled filminess of a lake in the autumn sunshine; an icy, still, frozen hawthorn branch, dripping its morning dew; a cluster of primroses hidden in the moss of a spring bank; a daffodil pushing through the gap between two concrete slabs, are all tiny glimpses. Sometimes we are led into moments of astonishing captivation: the endless banks of wild flowers carpeting the banks of woodland in the Auvergne; the sun going down over the sea in Cardigan Bay; the morning sun touching the mountain top of Ben More on the island of Mull, after a night of heavy rain. Everyone will have their own memories of moments of deep detachment from the ordinariness of life, when the reality of God's beauty and omnipresence burst in upon us. That is why it is so important to find times for recreation and observance outside the banality of day-to-day life. We are helped enormously when we find or are given opportunities to drink in the natural world and to see something of God through it.

I remember particularly the discovery of a lake in the Dordogne one early summer morning. The water was peaty and soft; the soil around was sandy and gentle. There were pine trees and firs and beech and oak growing in clumps around open glades. Heather and gorse rippled over banks. Wild flowers were scattered along the sides of the paths. Around the edge of the lake were carpets of water lilies with their flowers opening to the morning sunshine. Leaping from leaf to leaf, and croaking with delight and joy, were a myriad of frogs, alive, vigorous, intoxicated with life. It seemed that the whole creation was pulsating with promise. 'I will turn aside and see this great sight'.

An Indian bishop visiting this country was talking to a group of clergy about the experience of contrast between the Church of South India and the Church of England. With enormous courtesy and graciousness, he affirmed so much of the resources and the hospitality and the programmes and the architecture of the Church in the parishes as he had seen them. He paid tribute to the way in which a missionary Church had brought the Christian faith to his land. He spoke with a sense of awe of the social and welfare and medical provision in the United Kingdom. To him, he said, it seemed almost like a visible expression of the Kingdom of God, when he thought of the poverty and insecurity of so many in India.

Then he was pressed. Surely there must be areas of the life of the Church that he would criticise and which needed reform? He paused and looked up at some surrounding trees, for the meeting was in a garden. 'The fault to me', he said, 'the great fault of all you Western clergy is that you are always on the go. You are always rushing about. You all have

too much to do. Coming from the East, this worries me. You
must spend some time in the day when you are still. You
must watch a bird in flight. You must contemplate the leaf of
a tree. You must feel the touch of the grass'.

Perhaps part of the rejection of spiritual persuasion in
Western cultures is the enforced detachment of so many from
daily contact with natural beauty, from animals, from opportunities to see and touch natural things. A parish community
must seek ways of facilitating travel and spaces and the use
of retreat houses and accessibility to parks and gardens. It
was the challenge of the bush aglow with the glory of God
which brought Moses, in the silence of the desert, and in the
anxiety of his experience of violence, into an encounter with
a personal God.

The encounter is a real encounter. God calls Moses by
name as he will call each of us by name if we will listen to
his voice. Indeed, the importance of a name can never be
exaggerated. Some of us are better at remembering names
than others, but the struggle to know people by name should
be a corporate struggle of the Christian community. It identifies us. It gives us worth person to person. It transfers
between us what is given by God. Named, we are individually important and known. Children will always give any
creature, from a kitten to a fish, a name. It is adults who talk
in the generic about 'your cat', or 'your fish tank'. It is
through constant re-remembering, through a daily prayer
life, through a corporate sharing, that the knowledge of
names is built up. It is astonishing how often parish communities will know each other only like ships passing in the
night. 'Oh yes, the lady who sits at the front on the right'.
'The man with the stick'. 'The girl who wears the hat'. 'The
woman who smokes'. Moses, drawn by the sight of the bush,
encounters God who calls him by name. The experience, as
all encounters with God will be, is immensely humbling. The
ground is holy, his shoes must be taken off, he hides his face,
for he is afraid to look on God. This experience of awe, of
challenge, of unmasking reveals a truth about our own
encounters with God. Faced by his presence, by his personal

knowledge, by his involvement in our lives, by his one-to-one relationship, we become afraid.

In Kenneth Grahame's *The Wind in the Willows*, Rat and Mole take a boat journey down the river where they land upon an island, drawn by the sound of mystical Pan-pipe music. There, in the anthropomorphic vein of the story, they encounter a divine presence: 'A Friend and Helper', infinitely kind, reassuring and gentle, embracing a security and intensity of religious experience, complete with the incorporation of a baby otter sleeping peacefully at this 'Christ-figure's' feet.

In the moment of encounter, Mole turns to Rat: 'Rat!' he found breath to whisper, shaking, 'Are you afraid?' 'Afraid?' murmured the Rat, his eyes shining with unutterable love. 'Afraid of Him? Oh never, never! and yet - and yet - O, Mole, I am afraid!' Then the two animals, crouching to the earth, bowed their heads and did worship.[2] Fear is an ingredient in the encounter with God. In the dialogue which follows in the encounter, Moses perceives one of the contours of God. He is a God involved in the sufferings and afflictions of his people. He is a God of the past, the present and the future. He is a God who has no name for himself for he is who he is. He is a God who will act, who will enable, and who will commission. He is a God of faithfulness and of promise. He is a God who knows Moses by name.

In chapter 4, Moses seems to be stricken by a *'crise de nerfs'* at the reality of his call and there follows a peculiar play with rods becoming serpents and hands becoming leprous. If the account seems bizarre to us, it will probably be a truth of spiritual experience that God will invariably send us signs of hope and encouragement if we will seek to respond to his commissioning of us. Indeed at times of discouragement and personal insecurity and uncertainty it is positively hopeful to ask for and then to look out for the very signs of validation which God will give to us.

I can remember a week when I was faced with an agonising choice about embarking upon a completely new direction. After a week of arduous decision making, a new job

offer was accepted and, instead of a feeling of peace and
relief that the struggle was over, there came only a continued
sense of dither and lack of confidence. The unexpected
arrival at the door of a concerned friend with an extravagant
bunch of flowers and a card of encouragement, at personal
cost of time and money, became a sign not only of divine
assurance, but also a perception of the gift of women's ministry. What man would ever have affirmed a commissioning
in such a way?

Moses said to God: 'Who am I that I should go to Pharaoh
and bring the sons of Israel out of Egypt?'. But God said: 'I
will be with you ... and you shall serve God on this mountain'.[3]

In the great events of the story which is to unfold and in
which Moses will play such a crucial part, the Bible declares
that God involves himself at the deepest level. Again and
again the history described is a story in which God is per-
sonally engaged. The memory of it will become crucial to the
Jewish, and later the Christian, experience of faith. Moses
emerges as the great interpreter of the historical saga in
which the involvement of God will be such a vital ingredient.
The call of Moses is the beginning of the call to redemption.
Moses is called by name. His future lies in a personal relationship with God.

There is much in the human psyche which finds it hard to
believe that we are of any personal value or importance to
that distant power and energetic force which we call God.
We find it hard to rationalise the possibility that God could
be so remotely interested in us as to call us by name. Our
over-abundance of corporate or personal guilt makes it hard
to believe that we have an individual and personal worth so
precious to God that he may engineer means and opportunities for our turning aside to see him and to be called by him.
The Christian Gospel asserts that our value is such that God's
involvement in human destiny is so intimate and so closely
bound up in the divine hope, that the birth, death and resurrection of Jesus Christ is the consequence of God's personal
and individual concern.

Moses is called by God by name. He is commissioned, affirmed and sent. Such is the shape of God that he calls us aside, to do business with us, to make himself known, and to use us in the life-story of his world.

Jesus said: 'Are not two sparrows sold for a penny? and not one of them will fall to the ground without your Father's will ... Fear not, therefore; you are of more value than many sparrows'.[4]

Chapter 4

The Over-shadowing God:

Moses encounters the glory of God

(Exodus 33. 7–23)

MANY ARGUE that the patriarchal roots to Jewish faith and the stories which they contain, reinforce the concept of a masculine, authoritarian, distant God whose chief concern is to discipline and chasten his people. One of the faithful perceptions that emerges early in the book of Exodus is the concept of the 'over-shadowing' by God of his people. Soon after the great delivery from Pharaoh's horsemen, as the Red Sea parts, we are told that the presence of God appeared as a pillar of cloud by day and as fire by night. Furthermore, these two images were not to depart from the people. They were to be a sign of assurance, a token of divine presence.

The image of the pillar of cloud by day and of fire by night, picked up in the well-known hymn: 'Guide me O thou great redeemer', has its own mystical validity. God's call to the individual or to the community is not in itself an insurance of protection or reward. Curiously, within our human response to God lurks a strange search for approval and approbation or condemnation and punishment, depending on how we have judged ourselves.

So often, people afflicted by illness, tragedy or misfortune, believe themselves to be, at some level, responsible. Some may even endure stoically on the grounds of just retribution, real or imagined. In a more complicated way, there is a lurking hope, too, that faithfulness will produce its own reward, and a sense of injustice can emerge, if that expectation is not fulfilled. God is expected to act fairly and to deal justly in punishment and reward!

The experience of God, and of a relationship with him is not a guarantee for protection or fortification. Indeed, there are no guarantees in the human life-experience, although we go to some lengths to protect ourselves against the possibility of danger and to try to sow seeds for the harvest of personal recompense. The Exodus story speaks of a God who will go with his people, and who will over-shadow them and surround them. The image of the pillar of cloud by day and of the fire by night is an image of omnipresence, of in-dwelling, of enfolding. God's promise of faithfulness is a promise to surround, whatever may befall and however life's pattern may unfold.

By the 1st and 2nd centuries before Christ, Jewish rabbinic thought had crystallised this idea of the over-shadowing by God of his people, of his going before, of the constancy of his presence, into the idea of the Shekinah, from the Hebrew root word meaning 'to dwell'. This term has a feminine gender and there is a gentleness and feminine quality in the concept of God's constant, over-shadowing, enfolding and treasuring love. St Luke picks up the idea in his account of the Annunciation: 'the power of the most high shall over-shadow you'.[1]

The psalmist speaks of God holding him in the shadow of his tent[2], and in psalm 139 elaborates on the experience of being 'encompassed behind and before'. Julian of Norwich writes: 'For our soul is so deeply based in God, and so end-lessly treasured, that we cannot come to knowledge of it until we first have knowledge of God, who is the creator to whom it is one-ed'.[3]

In the encounter which is described in Exodus 33, some-thing of this feminine, enfolding quality of the shape of God is experienced. The context is one of despair and set-back. Having renewed the covenant relationship with God on the mountain, Moses is thought to have been too long about his prayers, and on his return he is met by the apostasy of the worship of the golden calf. Aaron seems to be an equivocal figure, and at this juncture to have been easily persuaded to revert to pagan practices in the people's search for a 'God who will go with us'.

The text tells us that outside the camp, as a sign of the dis-pleasure with which God had received the people's apostasy, had been set the tent of meeting. This holy shrine carrying the ark of the covenant, the wooden chest which held the

stones of the ten commandments, and which was the original throne of the invisible God, was the place where Moses
would meet God face to face and speak to him as a man
speaks to his friend.

There is a sense of validity about this early story of a
prayer life, which compels us to search for our own 'tent of
meeting', where we can meet God face to face. Part of the
tragedy of modern life is the inevitability of locked churches
and closed corners. We all need our 'place' to talk to God as
a man talks to his friend. We have to try to find such a place
and make it our own. The daily worship in the chapel of a
parish church can be such a help in the availability of a time
and a place to encounter God in a 'tent of meeting'.

The story comes in varying forms of the inadequate parish-
ioner who was observed by his parish priest entering the
parish church every day at the same time and sitting quietly
in a manner which seemed to be engaging with little. When
asked what he said in his prayers, the answer was: 'I looks at
Him and He looks at me'. The Lord used to speak to Moses
face to face as a man speaks to his friend.

Outside the tent of meeting, as a sign of the reality of God's
presence, would rest the pillar of cloud. It would become the
symbol of the presence. It would be the signal for individual
worship and affirmation, for was not this the signal of the
binding relationship between God and his people? Was not
the pillar of cloud by day and the fire by night a seal, a sacrament, a sign of the promise and the faithfulness of God?

In the tiny village church of Hinton Ampner, south of Win-
chester, a memorial east window has been set which depicts,
in the columns of the window lights, the pillar of cloud and
a spiral of fire. It is an unusual choice for coloured window
glass and there cannot be many other windows of the kind.
I visited the church entirely by chance at a time of complex
decision-making, and at random, for my purpose in visiting
the village was to see the National Trust gardens, not the
church. At the time, the symbolic window seemed to say
something unexpected and graphic about the promise to
Moses in the complexity of the rebellion of a 'stiff-necked

people', as he communed in the tent of meeting. 'I know you by name, and you have also found favour in my sight ... my presence will go with you and I will give you rest'.[4]

Like so many of us, Moses grapples in the dark with the uncertainty of the message, and with the complicated dangers of the future. He searches for approval and for reassurance. It is the search of the faithful for the tangible from the intangible. Remarkably, it is so often part of the contour of God that at so many cross-road junctures in our lives, he will send us the very sign and signal for which we grope. Only if our lives have found a rhythm and pattern that takes the use of our own tent of meeting seriously will we be alert to the signals when they come. Part of the practice of the spiritual life involves keeping in alert order the receiver mechanism, for the signals which will be sent.

Moses calls for a vision of God's glory, and in the richness of his encounter with God, that glory is shown. Somewhere in the barren mountains of the Sinai desert, Moses is brought face to face with God. He is to be hidden in a cleft of the rock, hidden as it were in the womb of the earth, and the glory of God is to pass by. The glory is somehow to be expressed in the promise of God to be faithful in his graciousness and mercy, albeit selective, for the shape of the glory will demand a holy response. In the mystical language of the encounter, the face of God will not be disclosed for no one can see God's face and live. Moses is to be covered by the hand of God, overshadowed by the Shekinah, enclosed by the love and the presence of the God who accompanies our every journey and our feeble struggles. Hidden in the cleft, enclosed by the hand, the glory is to pass by, and the vision of the back of God is to be disclosed when the hand is lifted.

It is a reality of our experience that the vision of God will be authenticated with a curious opaqueness. Our own encounters can so often seem to be like seeing the back of God and not his face. Like Jacob and his dream of the ladder, the glory passes by. We reach to grasp it and it is gone. The reality is like waking from a good dream in which we have been deeply asleep, like straining for the sound of music on a distant hill, or scanning the horizon for a vision of sunshine that has dipped behind a cloud. It is from our yearning and our longing that our search for God begins. It is out of that yearning and longing that we glimpse God's back, but his face shall not be seen. Gerard Manley Hopkins grasps some of this sense of longing in his poem: *The Wreck of the Deutschland*. In the poem, the poet tries to make sense of the wreck off the Kent coast on 7 December 1875 of the German registered schooner, *Deutschland*, bound for America. Among the passengers are five Franciscan nuns. One of these calls out from the tumult and horror as the ship goes down: 'Oh Christ, come quickly' and the poet picks up the longing for redemption, hope, meaning, unity, and for understanding of the purposes of God in the tragedy. This disaster seems, in its pathos, to bring some sense of divine encounter upon the English shore because of the faithfulness of the nuns:

> 'Dame, at our door
> Drowned, and among our shoals,
> Remember us in the roads, in the heaven-haven of the
>   Reward:
> Our King back, oh, upon English souls!
> Let him easter in us, be a day spring to the dimness of
>   us,
> Be a crimson-cresseted east,
> More brightening her, rare-dear Britain, as his reign
>   rolls,
> Pride, rose, prince, hero of us, high-priest,
> Our hearts' charity's hearth's fire, our thoughts'
>   chivalry's throng's Lord'.[5]

Enclosed, enfolded, hidden, affirmed, yearning, longing, Moses encounters God in the depth of himself as the glory passes by. It is our hope and opportunity that we can be shown the glory of God as it enfolds and envelopes us in the complexity of our own earthly pilgrimages of hope.

Once, I journeyed into the ancient city of Petra, in Jordan, the remarkable post-Roman centre of civilisation built and civilised by the Nabataean Arabs. The site is an extensive and intact centre of very remarkable human living, surrounded by its own fortress of hills, which is why it remained undiscovered and not invaded for so long. In the still clarity of a November day, I climbed up above the ruined Byzantine monastery whose civilisation supplanted the Nabataeans. I came to an area of deserted rockland, passing a family of Bedouin camped in a cave. They seemed to be without any form of modern aids to life, except a battery powered television with an aerial swinging above the rocks!

Further on was a place of very great stillness, with a view stretching over the Jordanian mountains, not a million miles from the Sinai to the south where Moses had been hidden in his cleft. As I watched the occasional bird hovering against the brilliance of the blue sky and felt the stillness and silence of this isolated place, it seemed as if a strange wind picked up the emptiness and swooped across the landscape ahead filling the area with a presence that was both formidable and yet reassuring. In psalm 18 the psalmist writes of God coming swooping upon the wings of the wind, and, in verse 10, of parting the heavens and coming down, with darkness under his feet.[6] In the craggy stillness and black rockiness of the Jordanian mountain range, I grasped something of the vision of the early desert poets and interpreters, who, out of the strength of their oral tradition, could picture the nature of an encounter with God set against the backcloth of the mountains and sands of the Arabian deserts.

The contour of God shown to Moses was one of power, of assurance, of enclosure, of accompaniment. It was formidably demanding and yet infinitely reassuring. We will often seem to be hidden in clefts while the glory of God passes by and we are shown his back but not his face. His nature is both hidden and initiatory. As we travel each on our own particular pathway to the future, his promise is of over-shadowing and of cover.

At the end of St Matthew's gospel, Jesus leads his disciples out to another mountain, at another time, and in another place. There is the same disparity between faith and doubt which seems to have beset the Israelite escapers. The risen Christ empowers his disciples with that authority and sense of purpose which is the validation of the early Church. Out of the depth of that Church's experience are heard the words: 'And lo, I am with you always, to the close of the age'.[7]

Chapter 5

The Enabling God:

The Commissioning of Joshua

(Joshua 1. 1–9)

AT THE POINT on Mount Nebo where Moses is alleged to have died, a cross, cunningly intertwined to correlate to the rod on which Moses lifted up the serpent in Numbers 21, stands silhouetted against the sky. Dropping sharply beneath is an escarpment, prelude to a breathtaking view of the whole of the Jordan valley, and in the distance the city of Jericho. Here is the promised land flowing with milk and honey, still to western eyes harshly barren and stony, and today such a recent symbol of the rigidity of international relations, as scattered intervals of barbed wire mark the Jordanian/Israeli frontier as it weaves its way across the open land, soon perhaps to be replaced by a more regular frontier.

Here, at this point of spectacular vision, with the lushness of the Jordan valley contrasting with the harshness of the uplands, Joshua is presumed to have received his commission to continue the leadership of Moses under an encounter of divine instruction.

The book of Joshua was written probably during the reign of King Josiah some thirty years before the fall of Jerusalem in 587 BC. The author is likely to have been involved in writing parts, if not all, of the book of Deuteronomy and there are a number of literary and historical parallels. The author is concerned to find the roots and tell the history of his people in the light of perilous contemporary affairs. He is searching for divine authentication of the Israelite tradition. For him, there has to be a triumphalist quality to his account. Much of the rest of the book of Joshua is horribly blood-thirsty and intransigent.

Despite the subsequent violence, Joshua's encounter with God does reveal to us something deep about the contour of God as we can come to know him and be enabled by him. Joshua may be portrayed by the Deuteronomic author as an

29

heroic clone of Moses, but the text still unfolds for us perceptions about the nature of God's contractual methods in
leading and underwriting our lives. The strange cross at
Mount Nebo with its entwined, serpentine tentacles, teaches
us about the shape of a God, who, out of his love and sense
of purpose, entwines himself into our future. He leaves us
free to make our own choices, but his will is indefatigable in
enabling and leading each of us into making our story contributory to the building up of his rule, what Jesus was to
call: The Kingdom of God.

The text tells us that Joshua was given clear instructions
by God for his own and his people's future. He was to be the
leader of the people, military commander, and heir apparent
to Moses. Most people's experience runs contrary to that
which the author reports Joshua as enjoying. Far from giving clear instructions, God frequently seems to be hazy and
indefinite in the way in which he reveals what we have come
to call: 'God's purpose'.

Earlier generations in our Christian tradition tended to see
the nature of God as working through a 'Divine Plan', believing that God has a vision for us all, a journey mapped for us.
According to this perception the task of the discerning
Christian is to attune him or herself to this overriding design.
In this endeavour, the challenge will be one of counsel and
interpretation; how to decipher and comprehend the contours of the divine map; how to match our will to God's will;
how to integrate our futures to God's all-encompassing master plan.

This methodology served in its day, for it is surely true that
God is quite unlimited in the varying manner in which he
shows his face. In the maturity of today's Christian era, our
perception calls us into making our own map. Personal freedom, if that is indeed what we have, requires us to make our
own decisions and to abide by them.

We are limited in our capacity to be free to choose by a
range of varying restrictions of culture and upbringing, of
education and influence, of individual experience in child-
hood or adolescence, but God calls us into the maturity of

decision-making. We are not puppets dancing to a divine tune, and God is no master puppeteer pulling a multitude of strings with whose colour and twitch we are asked to engage. In our mature spiritual life we are free agents faced, very often, with a plethora of complex and complicated choices, in which the varying demands of self-interest, the interests of others and the demands of our faith, make a series of competing demands.

It is with this maturity that God will involve himself not as a Mister Fixit, absolving us from the responsibility of our own decision-making, but as that presence which enables and strengthens us into making useful and self-fulfilling conclusions out of whatever decisions we, on our own responsibility, make for ourselves. No decision made, however disastrous the consequences may seem to us to have become, is beyond the enabling capacity of God to make things well. Perhaps that was part of Julian of Norwich's understanding when she describes in her visions the expectation that: 'All shall be well, and all manner of things shall be well'.[1] At one level, her faith can seem like the parrot-cry of foolish optimism, for who knows what will work out ahead and what will not? At a deeper level, Julian expresses the confidence of the faithful that whatever befalls, and however foolishly we may have plundered our lives, God's capacity to enable recovery and purpose is never thwarted. Joshua's call to service and command is untrammelled by any uncertainty. He has to make a personal decision. He is ordered into leadership and he responds.

The instructions which he is given do, nonetheless, contain a series of reminders which teach us something about the contours of God. They clarify the nature of the enterprise. The people are to cross the Jordan in order to receive the gift of land, and land in quantity. Much more land is named than is ever in fact to be forthcoming. Even the most right-wing of Israel's politicians has never claimed land as far north as the Euphrates. In line with the great Pentateuchal theme that the people are to be led into a promised land and rewarded with a country of their own, with all the violence and injustice which is implied, there is within the promise a sense in which God promises Joshua reward and success. In the light of the teaching of Jesus, this kind of blandishment needs much re-interpretation.

The teaching of Jesus reiterates again and again that reward and blessing will be found not through the traditional expectations, but through loss and failure and sacrifice and death. To lose your life is to find it. To depart from known security is to discover a new and much richer security. To give all away is to find a new inheritance vastly richer than all that has been lost. The teaching could be summed up in Mark 8. 35: 'For whoever would save his life will lose it; and whoever loses his life for my sake and the Gospel's will save it'.[2]

Even seen through spectacles coloured by the teaching of Jesus, the element of reward is held out as a clear expecta-tion ahead for whoever will faithfully follow a search for God. For Joshua, the affirmation is unequivocal: 'No man shall be able to stand before you all the days of your life'.[3]

It is within the Christian persuasion that part of the con-tour of God is a contour that is enabling and fortifying. One of the enormous privileges of the parish priest and indeed of every minster, ordained or lay, is to stand close to people at the interception of their lives, at moments of great trauma and difficulty as well as at moments of joy and success. Inevitably, the former loom the largest for it is at times of stress and difficulty, of failure and illness, of loss and tragedy that we are at our most vulnerable and our most dependent. Again and again it seems that God, in the words of the psalmist: 'reaches down from on high and takes us, drawing us out of the great waters'.[4] One of the great blessings of the last twenty years has been the rediscovery of the ministry of healing. This ministry can be expressed in so many ways, through counselling, through friendship, through the laying on of hands, through anointing, through services of healing, through prayer. Backed by medical counsel and advice, spir-itual healing and change is often timely given. At its best, a faith community is itself an agent of healing, not least in its ministry of welcome.

The enabling God promises Joshua success and reward. If the character of that success and reward seems to us uncomfortably self-interested and gilded, it would be a truth of the contour of God that we are given not only what we need, but more abundantly, when we respond to his will and capacity to reach out to us in our dependence. It is probable that part of Joshua's capacity to receive from God was to be found in his sense of personal inadequacy in taking over from the charismatic leadership of Moses.

'As I was with Moses, so I will be with you.'[5] A large part of the Old Testament story is a story of the reminder of what God has done in the past. Much of the poetry, and of the teaching of the psalms is a re-run of the great deeds of God in the history of the people, particularly the delivery from slavery in Egypt. It can sometimes feel, in 20th century terms, an astonishing piece of folk memory, to recite at evening prayer, after a hard day on hospital wards, or comforting the family of a sick child, or burying a young accident victim, or counselling a sufferer from AIDS, psalm 105, for example, the reminder of those ancient events. It has its own curious purpose.

When we are faced with situations of daunting and terrifying insecurity, it is very easy to doubt God's capacity to act. 'My sister returned from hospital this morning with the news that she has secondary cancer in the lymph glands.' 'The company for which I have worked for twenty years has been forced into liquidation and we are told that there are no funds even for redundancy payments.' 'My daughter is inextricably involved with an unprincipled married man whose motivation is plain for all but her to see.' 'Our son has died from a cot death, and my wife was told that she would be unlikely to conceive again.' 'My hip needs a third replacement, but I am warned that my bones have crumbled too seriously for another repair.'

It is a necessary part of discerning the contour and shape of God to allow oneself to be reminded again and again of what he has done in the past. Every individual journey needs its own travelogue. In the past, there have been staging posts.

In the diary of many people's lives there have been oases and resting places. 'When I was hard-pressed, He came to my rescue'.[6] Certainly there may have been times of great sorrow and deep suffering but it is the experience of faith that it is precisely within those periods of darkness and wilderness that God's faithfulness is made plain. 'As I was with Moses so I will be with you, I will not fail you nor forsake you.'[7] It is important never to forget what God has done in the past for the past points to the surety of God to be God in the present and the future. The contour of God is enabling in time of challenge, and faithful in the story of the past.

Two further conditions are given to Joshua in the commissioning he receives and which are to be part of the endeavour on which he is bound: Courage and commitment to the Law.

Courage is a quality which the contours of God ask of us. It is not an easy virtue, for most of us are easily panicked and intimidated by forces which seem superior to ourselves. Those with spiritual perception will tend to be people with a sense of the value of others, and unlikely to be forceful and overbearing in their relationships. It is easy to be manoeuvred into being manipulated and overwhelmed. No doubt Joshua felt his own sense of insecurity and personal cowardice, as he faced the responsibility of command and the certainty of the intrigues of leading personalities in the tribal hierarchy, who would have been jealous of his new position. 'Be strong and of a good courage; be not frightened neither be dismayed; for the Lord your God is with you wherever you go.'[8]

That contour of God which calls forth courage and resolution from us is one which promises an enabling strength and vitality in all the encounters and conflicts of our daily lives. Many will have had the experience of facing intimidating and dangerous situations only to discover that the strength of the Holy Spirit of God provided a sustaining and fortifying strength.

The second condition for Joshua was to be the observance of the law of Moses. The Mosaic Law was a crucial ingredient in the social cohesion of the tribal community, and the

Deuteronomic author of the book would have valued it as an historical platform for the reforms of Josiah's reign. In the Christian story, the Mosaic Law is both strength and weakness. Its social provisions are so endemically part of west European law, as to make it hard to conceive of any basis of a morally ordered society without heed to its strictures. Part of the tragedy of modern western society is to have lost touch with the spirit of the legal provisions, so that the social fabric of community tears at the seams. For Jesus, the law was to be fulfilled, not abolished, and his claims to teach that fulfilment by spirit and not by letter was a root cause of his clash with Pharisaic authority.

The contour and shape of the enabling God demands of us allegiance to principle and a moral code which it may be hard to set in tablets of stone, but which are essential ingredients in the conditional contract by which we enter our own particular promised land. In a society where many of the moral traditions have broken down it is easy for people with overt Church allegiances to defend courses of action which defy the Mosaic code. Many of the moral decisions which Christians are called to make today are fraught with temptations and complex value judgements. In the shape of the enabling God who would lead Joshua into the fulfilment of promise, there is an absoluteness about the condition of commitment to the law which challenges the faithful to a constant re-examination of motive, action, and desire. The experience of the power of God is that it can never leave hold of any opportunity, however fragmented, however morally craven, however disordered, to rebuild, re-enact, and reshape, dependent only on that sense of personal commitment which is the hallmark of the response of Joshua to his commission.

The story is told of how the great carpet-making families in Persia, Turkey and Asian Russia used to manufacture their magnificent products. The design and weave of a grand carpet was a matter for the extended family. Everyone was pressed into service from the old to the very young. It was a corporate and shared enterprise in which everyone, however feeble or inexperienced, had a part to play. The grand design of the carpet, its pattern and shape, would be in the mind of the head of the family. With him lay the ultimate responsibility for the finished product. In the process of the weave, with its enormously complex range of colour and pattern, and its multitude of tiny knots, all sorts of mistakes and imperfections would occur. Arthritic hands and blind eyes, tiny inexperienced fingers, over-calloused working hands would all contribute to set back, or falsify, the pattern. So skilled, so the story goes, was the Master Carpet Maker in his capacity to enable the design that, whatever mistake of pattern or dropped stitch or failed knot might occur, as the family community, both individually and corporately, set about their task, there was always a finished product where the mistakes had been gathered up into the perfection of the whole.

Perhaps too, there were two conditions required: courage and confidence to begin the enterprise; and allegiance, through the mistakes, to the basic rules of carpet-making, and all backed by the memory of the great carpet-making traditions and the skill and enterprise of the past.

Jesus said: 'As Moses lifted up the serpent in the wilderness, so must the Son of Man be lifted up, that whoever believes in Him may have eternal life'.[9]

'And I when I am lifted up from the earth, will draw all men to myself'.[10]

Chapter 6

The Playfulness of God:

The Call of Samuel

(1 Samuel 3. 1–14)

THE STORY of the call of Samuel has been reproduced in many different paintings over centuries. The story is rich with picture-language in which the old man and the young boy are held in tandem against a background of sin and disorder. In the text, Samuel's origins are painfully reconstructed. His father Elkanah is a man of faith and conviction. He is wont to sacrifice to God at the shrine at Shiloh once a year. He has two wives, one of whom, Hannah, is barren. His second wife, Peninnah, is particularly cruel and destructive because Hannah has no children. A picture is presented of the marginalisation of Hannah and of her suffering and loss of self-worth.

In her desperation she prays for a child, and, in a way which is reminiscent of all humanity's attempt to bargain with God, promises that she will offer the child to the Lord if she could be blessed with a baby. Thus it is that Samuel finds himself in the care of Eli at the shrine at Shiloh. There is pathos in the child's loss of home life and in the yearly visit which his mother makes to him, bringing him a little robe that she has made. The faithfulness and sense of thanks-giving in Hannah is expressed to God in a foretaste of the Magnificat: a recognition that it is God who gives, and that the giving will be to the weak, and the poor and the vulnerable. God will use weakness to confound strength.

So the young boy ministers at the shrine at Shiloh, under the tutelage of the priestly Eli, who, for all his sense of personal devotion, is unable to control the venality and corruption of his two sons: Hophni and Phineas. Tellingly, the Deuteronomic writer, at the beginning of his attempt to paint the story of Israel's greatness at a time of upheaval and challenge in the late 8th century BC, tells us that the word of the

37

Lord was rare or scarce in those days, that there was no frequent or open vision.

It is so often into times of spiritual aridity and sterility that the shape of God becomes moulded. It is almost as if periods of spiritual disadvantage become periods of insight and growth. A French priest working in an area of very great secularity in a house-church which few frequented, was asked why he continued; he replied that it was to keep the rumour of God alive. Today's world, for all its comparison with the description that 'the word of the Lord was rare in those days',[1], has seen its own burgeoning of new spiritual insight and vision, particularly in the development of places of pilgrimage and healing, such as Iona, Taizé, Lourdes, Haddington and Walsingham.

The words of the Chilean poet, Pablo Naruda, offer their own insight into the clarity of spiritual perception at times of general religious malaise:

'So that you may hear me
At times
My words get fainter and fainter,
Like the marks made by the seagulls on the sand'.[2]

In the darkness of the night and surrounded by the mystical presence of the ark, with the lamp of God still shining beside it, God calls Samuel by name and an encounter is made with the child. There is early confusion as to the nature of who is the caller. The clarity of the call is undoubted but in the first two stages it seems to the child that the call must come from Eli. When the encounter with God has been made the reality of the seriousness of the political, military and religious situation is made clear to the boy, who has, later, to face Eli with the revelation of what will befall as a consequence.

There is something curiously playful about the call of Samuel. There is something vulnerable about the boy and something vacillating and therefore unattractive about Eli. Unable, for all his prayers and religious observance, for all his rituals and cult ceremonies, to perceive the reality of the behaviour of his own family and his people, Eli becomes a type-cast of what can befall the religious mind. He is wedded into ceremony. He is blind in fact and name. He has preserved the outward form but has lost the inward validity. He has kept the letter of the law but has been compliant and acquiescent in selling short the keeping of the spirit of the law.

Eli stands for all time as a warning to all faithful people about the keeping of ceremony and observance of cult forms. Those who profess a spiritual perception and relate that to the forms and ceremonies of organised religious observance offer themselves as some kind of signpost to the world. Many who have been groping in the dark for some evidence of faith and of the finger of God at work in their lives may be very tender plants because of the tenuousness of their search. The exposure to organised religion may have a bewildering effect.

In a parish deeply committed to the Lenten observance of Ash Wednesday ashing, as an outward sign of penitence, a small group banded closely together in their determination to preserve the tradition when suggestions were made about other ways of expressing the Ash Wednesday renewal. In their insecurity at the fear of the loss of something that seemed precious to them, harsh criticisms were made of another group who wished to see Ash Wednesday kept in silence, fasting and vigil. At the end of the traditional ashing ceremony, there emerged the incongruity of one group complete with ashed crosses on their heads, criticising destructively, in the light of what they had received, those who would have preferred to make their observance in another way. Cultic ceremony brings with it its own sense of danger and misinterpretation.

Jesus' criticism of the Pharisees centred on their hypocrisy. Those who are called into a religious observance, however that may be expressed in local cultic or liturgical custom, will be exposed to the world around them. They will be looked to for signs of faithfulness, integrity and truth in the lifestyle of their religious observance.

The anomalous sight of worshippers who come out of

church and who walk home in the same direction, one on either side of the road, never speaking; or of families arguing as they enter cars after acts of worship; or of harsh disciplining of children after receiving the sacrament; all these raise their own spectre of Eli. The organised Church is bound to contain its own share of sexual infidelity, financial irregularity, displays of temper and competition, as in any other human community. What makes particular demands on Christian outward observance is the reality that that observance is a sign and signal to an unbelieving world. Faith is caught not taught, and Eli, faithful in his prayers, but blind to the venality of his sons, stands out as a warning and an example.

It is part of the contour of God to respond to such a situation in early Israel with the playful call to Samuel. The tribal confederacy has settled itself into a homeland and, although surrounded by military and religious threat, has established its own regional identity under a series of charismatic leaders known as Judges. One of the last of these will be the prophet Samuel. Before his full role will be able to be developed, disasters of a terrible kind lie in wait for the tribes. The ark will be captured. Philistine aggrandisement will be a real threat. The response to his vulnerability will be the call for a king to unite the confederacy and to act as a military leader.

Before all this can come to pass, the child Samuel receives an encounter with God. It befalls in the stillness of the night, in the gentle twilight of the late evening, in the shadowy mysteriousness of the Shiloh sanctuary, near the great symbol of the presence of God: the ark of the covenant itself.

The text tells us that Samuel is convinced that he has been called. He is initially certain that the call comes from Eli, and indeed it is Eli who must interpret to Samuel the conviction that the call is not from man but from God. The call is definite and, once responded to, Samuel in his youthfulness must become the messenger for tidings that are a heavy load for young shoulders. What contour for God can we deduce from the story of this midnight call?

First of all, there is this curiously playful element to the initial encounter. God calls Samuel three times, and while the message is for Eli and a wider world, it is through a child that God will speak. Very little in the Bible speaks of a sense of humour in the divine revelation and very little in the story of Jesus which points to the comical, though it is clear that the table fellowship with publicans and sinners certainly involved much that was convivial, light-hearted and probably funny.

In our perception of God, a playful contour must be part of the encounter. It is so tempting to take ourselves too seriously. It is so easy to become obsessed with the minutiae of our own problems and anxieties. It is so easy to see the life of organised religion as of such serious consequence as to lose its comical side or, as happens more often, for the funny side to be missed, and the unfunny side to be the joke.

There is a playfulness in the God who calls a young boy three times and watches him scurry off to the old man whose blindness is the heart of the problem. There is a playfulness about the use of a child to reveal the future, even if that playfulness merges into a new authoritarianism when the strictures of the punishment in store are laid out. There is a playfulness in the contour of God as he laughs with us and about us in the chances and changes of our lives, our petty anxieties, our foolish fears, our taking of ourselves too seriously.

Secondly, the encounter by the child Samuel in the Shiloh sanctuary reveals something of God that will be true always. Again and again, God uses the poor and the weak, the young and the unlikely, to confound the rich and the strong. Samuel's mother Hannah had sung a Magnificat-like hymn of praise when she heard that her prayers had been answered.

> 'He raises the poor from the dust;
> He lifts the needy from the ash-heap,
> to make them sit with princes
> and inherit a seat of honour.'[3]

So is pre-figured that great divine initiative which would in years to come seek out Mary at Nazareth and invite her into a response which would change the world. Mary's 'yes' to that invitation would become the 'yes' of all that is weak and marginalised about the human condition, in response to the will of God to use the humble and confound the mighty.

In the town of Sümeg in Southern Hungary there lies a medieval castle, now in semi-ruins. The castle was built at the top of a prominent hill, and can only be reached by a long climb. Every other year, in the courtyard of the castle, a Passion play is performed by a cast of some seventy Hungarian players, from children to old people. There is much in the play which resembles the medieval mystery plays in the York or Lincoln cycles. Much is uniquely Hungarian. Like the mystery plays, although the Passion is a key dimension to the drama, the story begins with the birth of Jesus and includes a number of events from the Gospel narrative.

The play is the Christ-event seen through Hungarian eyes. This means that there is much that relates to the Hungarian experience of the loss of empire and independence, and which reveals the experience of suffering and tyranny. As the narrative unfolds, the moment at which the authorities turn against Jesus is a scene where he begins to clown. He gathers round him a group of children and, dressing in a chaplet of flowers, laughs and plays the buffoon. All his previous sense of majesty and authority has become subordinate to a sense of childlike playfulness, romping, joking, acting the fool. It is this that turns an accusatory establishment against him, not the teaching about the Law.

At the end, in Revelation 86 of Julian's book, she seeks to make some sense of the complexity of sin and of the human condition and of the secret of Divine Providence. She struggles to find 'Our Lord's meaning'. The ultimate solution to the search is not fully revealed until the final revelation when she sees the ultimacy of the power of God's love.

'Woulds't thou know thy Lord's meaning in this thing? Be well aware: love was His meaning. Who showed it thee? Love. What showed He thee? Love. Why did He show it thee? For Love.'[4]

Before that conclusion, in Revelation 51, the longest of the revelations, a parable vision is revealed and explained. The parable is about a lord and a servant. With the background of late medieval England as the source of the picture, we are told of how the lord sits, and how the servant stands, of what they wear and of the contrast of the clothes, of the nature of their body language. The lord is depicted in his repose and peace and his sense of being, his passivity; the servant in his eagerness and spontaneous zeal to do his lord's bidding, his activity. The servant sets off to fulfil his lord's bidding, particularly, it transpires, to cultivate a special and welcome food, as a gardener. In his eagerness, leaping and running to fulfil the task, the servant falls desperately and painfully. The language and the image all have a droll and comical side. In the story of Julian's Revelation, the fall of the servant, who begins by representing Adam and then becomes a revelation of Christ, 'falls into the maiden's womb'.[5] The chapter expresses something of the doctrine of the Incarnation and then of the Resurrection. In the quaint language of Julian's writing, a picture is painted of a God lovingly looking on at the tragedy of the fall, allotting no blame and indeed 'constantly watching him most tenderly'.[6] The interaction, unity, is a Trinitarian perception of divine 'repose and peace'. The parable seems to present a picture of God looking on in detached involvement while the game of the story of Redemption is played out.

In C S Lewis' The Lion, the Witch and the Wardrobe there is a powerful scene when Aslan, the Lion, and Christ-figure, is restored to life after the dreadful events which led, at the hands of the white witch's magic, to his capture, binding and death. The story depicts a resurrection scene, in the early dawn, when a multitude of mice begin to nibble the cords which bind Aslan. The stone table upon which Aslan has been tied breaks in two, and Aslan stands shining in the sunrise, shaking his mane.

' "Oh, children," said the lion, "I feel my strength coming back to me. Oh, children, catch me if you can!". He stood for a second, his eyes very bright, his limbs quivering, lashing himself with his tail. Then he made a leap high over their heads and landed on the other side of the table. Laughing, though she did not know why, Lucy scrambled over to reach him. Aslan leaped again. A mad chase began. Round and round the hill-top he led them, now hopelessly out of their reach, now letting them almost catch his tail, now diving between them, now tossing them in the air with his huge and beautifully velveted paws and catching them again, and now stopping unexpectedly so that all three of them rolled over together in a happy laughing heap of fur and arms and legs. It was such a romp as no one has ever had except in Narnia.' [7]

In the bewilderment and unpredictability of our lives, it is easy to build a picture of a God who plays with us as a cat plays with a mouse. It can seem that blessings are given and withheld, that punishments are meted out or rescinded. This picture will produce its own distortion of the contour of a God who in the words of Julian of Norwich has love as his meaning. The distortion is the product of our own incapacity to deal easily with success and failure, with good times and bad, with times of joy as well as times of sorrow.

The playfulness of God is a playfulness that allows for parameters and safety nets, which searches us out in our follies and isolations and seeks for ways to restore us and rebuild us. It is the kind of playfulness that reaches out to a child in the mysterious dimness of the late night sanctuary at Shiloh, which sees him trotting back and forth three times, bemused at the nature of the God whom he did not yet know. If there is a severity and harshness in the message which Samuel is asked to convey to Eli, it is nothing less than the inevitable self-inflicted consequence of Eli's inability or lack of resolve in dealing with the hypocrisy of his sons. At the end of Chapter 3 we are told that 'Samuel grew and the Lord was with him and let none of his words fall to the ground'. [8] The mysterious night-time encounter, which called Samuel into a relationship with God, established a new chapter in the history of the Jewish people. Samuel stands as the last of the great prophetic judges bridging the confederacy of the past with the monarchic structure of the future. The story which unfolds is rich with success and failure, faithfulness and apostasy. Within the skeins of our equivocal lives, there is a sense in which part of the contour of God is one which plays games of joy and hope within the muddle of our faulty decision-making and self-interest. There is both detachment and involvement. There is a sharing in the game of life with its mixture of tragedy and pathos, as well as of hope and promise. Samuel, so playfully called, will become an instrument of the grace of God, though he himself is tragically doomed to repeat the mistakes of Eli, in his inability to control his own sons.

There is a part of the contour of God which will turn upside down the values and expectations of the world, which will use a child to convey a message to an old and experienced man, which will reveal in a baby born in homeless conditions, the reality of his power, which will enter into the snakes and ladders of the game of our lives, and will, by playing alongside us, show us something of his power.

Jesus said, rejoicing in the Holy Spirit, 'I thank thee, Father, Lord of heaven and earth, that thou has hidden these things from the wise and understanding and revealed them to babes; yea, Father, for such was thy gracious will'.[9]

Chapter 7

The God of Delivery:

David overcomes Goliath
(1 Samuel 17. 12–54)

THE ACCOUNT of David's victory with sling and stones against
the well-armed Philistine champion Goliath is a story of traditional heroism. All the biblical features of the conflict
between good and evil are woven together by the historian
of the books of Samuel. His authorship has a clear bias. The
events which the writer describes happened about the year
1020 BC. Writing later than this; he may have used contemporary sources and accounts preserved in the Davidic court.
The author's slant is clear; David is an heroic manifestation
of the spirit of God at work in the successful and triumphant
emergence of Israel's Golden Age. The events of the first
book of Samuel describe a transitional period when the traditional tribal confederacy gives way to an emerging centralised monarchy.

Saul, the first Israelite king, is an equivocal figure, chosen
in the tradition of the judges as a man of charisma and
stature, who will offer leadership and military skill at a time
of dangerous threat from the Amalekite tribes and the
iron-smelting Philistines. It is a watershed period in Israelite
history, as the old methods of tribal government are transformed into a monarchic system. The prophet Samuel stands
as a complex overseer of these transitional times. He appears
to sanction the anointing of Saul reluctantly.[1] Indeed, Saul
seems to be a hesitant king,[2] and the development of his psychological state of mind, as he becomes increasingly
depressed and paranoid, makes him but a partially satisfac-
tory choice.

In terms of Israelite self-understanding, the anointing of
Saul as king is a major change. Up to this point, the Lord has
been seen as king; and the charismatic leaders, judges and
military commanders, have gained their authority only because of the spirit of the Lord conferred upon them. Indeed it

is because 'the spirit of the Lord will come mightily upon'[3] Saul that he is anointed. If this is the spiritual justification, there is a more pressing and urgent military requirement, as the tribes seek to consolidate their position, surrounded by alien culture and aggressive competition. Saul has the stature and the bearing,[4] and it is hoped that he has the military skill.

The setting of the story of David and Goliath is rich with the nuances of the writer's recognition of Saul's military, spiritual and charismatic decline, and the emergence of David as the 'golden warrior' who will lead Israel into a time of stability and prosperity. The challenge of the Philistine champion is a trial of strength, which Saul and his armies are unable to combat. Goliath is representative of all that threatens Israelite security. His bronze armaments are a statement about Philistine metallurgy.[5] David triumphs in the best kind of heroic 'Boy's Own' tradition. His victory propels him into an opportunity for advancement and success. Indeed, he has already been anointed as the heir, for the spirit of the Lord had departed from Saul.[6]

There are those who find the Old Testament stories so heavily laden with violence and bloodshed as to be unacceptable to a meaningful understanding of God in today's world. Indeed the account of Saul's sparing of some of the flocks of the Amalekite king Agag[7] and the approbation which this invites from Samuel, seems incomprehensible in our search for a contour and shape of God which will speak today. For a period, Old Testament stories were discarded from the syllabuses of Sunday School teaching. It is the rediscovery of the power of the story, as a means of conveying the corporate memory, in the spiritual search for God, which can open up new windows of insight.

In the mid-60s I knew an old ex-Chief Petty Officer, Royal Navy. He was always immensely smart in his dress and used to salute me, whenever we met, in mock seriousness. His faith was deep and real. As a young sailor he had served at the battle of Jutland. He had been in the gun turret of a capital ship which had received a direct hit. He had seen several of his shipmates decapitated by flying metal. On the morning of the battle, he had prayed for delivery, and believed that he had received it. He may well have pictured God as an extra special Admiral-in-Chief, but his conviction was un-wavering. God, in his view, was a deliverer. What is more, the evidence of that theology of delivery lay for him in Old Testament stories.

I knew him at a time when television was only just becoming the norm in every home. My old sailor friend believed that the stories we would see on television would never rival the richness of the stories from the Old Testament, on which he had been brought up as a child in Sunday School! and which had moulded his faith.

The story of the conflict between David and Goliath is rich in a perception of delivery. In Johannine thought, the great contrasting themes of the challenge to darkness by light are a recurrent feature of the fourth gospel. In Pauline thought, the contrast between the life of the flesh and the life of the spirit have another primacy. In this story, Goliath is representative of all that is foreboding, intimidating, scornful and death-dealing. David, with his bright eyes,[8] his ordinary shepherd's clothes, and his five smooth stones, carefully selected from the brook,[9] is representative of that simple vitality and faithfulness which is a prerequisite to an interception with the power of God. Despite the bloodthirsty rhetoric, the key to David's faithfulness lies in his words: 'for the battle is the Lord's and he will give you into our hand'.[10]

The history of the Christian Church contains a catalogue of accounts of the attempt by one military power block after another to use God as the justification for the rightness of the cause and as the instrument of victory. It is a tattered and damaging backcloth to a search for the contours of God.

In times of acute danger and fear, very many people find themselves calling upon a force beyond themselves to rescue and deliver. There would be many testimonies to the answer to that call. My old Naval friend was quite clear that he had been delivered, and there was no purpose in asking why other shipmates had not been so preserved.

The author of the first book of Samuel believed, too, that

David's triumph over Goliath had been a delivery at the hand of God. He saw it moreover as evidence for the justification for the emergence of a new monarchic state in which the theocratic confederacy would give way to rule by the 'Lord's anointed'. For a long period in West European history, such ideas about divine kingship influenced greatly the course of events.

People will interpret their own deliveries in their own way. If God is real and important in the intricacy and minutiae of our lives, his will to respond to our emergencies will be real and effective .If the story speaks of David's delivery, it speaks also of the method by which that is achieved. The use of the small and the weak and the insignificant is, in the story, a crucial contrast to the power and armament of Goliath's accoutrements. It is an axiom of the Christian Church's life that the poverty of resource and the insignificance of available skill is no barrier to the advancement of the kingdom. On the contrary, it is often the very weakness of the body which is its strength. At St Paul puts it: 'For consider your call, brethren; not many of you were wise according to worldly standards, not many were powerful, not many were of noble birth; but God chose what is foolish in the world to shame the wise, God chose what is weak in the world to shame the strong'.[11]

The story teaches not only about an experience of personal delivery but also about the kind of resources which are likely to be effective. Christian communities in their present day struggle for money, adherents and support are often myopic about the vitality that can be available within. Churches with wealth and resource can find it more difficult to enhance their spiritual life, to be generous and outgoing, than those who by having little can offer much. Tiny Christian communities, in their fragility, have the opportunity to band together in a sense of common purpose, which can thus avoid the interest in inter-personal competitiveness which creeps so easily into the affairs of larger communities of human beings.

It is a tragedy if a small community feels beleaguered and defensive when it may have within it the opportunity for the

vitality of being the little flock to whom the Father has chosen to give the kingdom.[12] A sense of deeply inter-related
common purpose can be its own equivalent of the five
smooth stones from the brook. Truly committed unitedness
is by no means always a feature of Christian communities,
but the opportunities for discovering it can be greater among
small congregations.

The story of David and Goliath teaches us that one of the
contours of God is to receive delivery at a time of personal
and frightening threat. It teaches, too, that the resource for
that delivery is often both within and nearby. The story does
not solve the question as to why delivery is sometimes available and sometimes not.

In 1994, there has been much corporate thanksgiving for
the delivery on 6 June 1944 through the D-Day landings,
which freed France from German occupation; and in 1995
for the end of the war. The course of history might have been
different if another attempt at delivery on 20 July 1944 had
been successful.

Prior to that day, a number of Germans, including committed and devoted Christians, had joined a conspiracy to
assassinate Hitler, and so bring to an end the Second World
War. It is uncertain whether Winston Churchill's war cabinet
would have agreed peace terms with a post-Nazi government, but the conspirators believed that there was an
absolute need to remove Hitler from power. In theological
circles, there was debate as to whether tyrannicide could be
seen as a legitimate act of moral principle. Indeed a series of
conspiracies and plots had been discussed and activated since
the mid-30s.

Mary Bosanquet describes in The Life and Death of Dietrich Bonhoeffer the evolution of the thinking of this deeply
respected participant and esteemed Christian pastor, and theo-
logian: 'Though Bonhoeffer did not see Hitler as Anti-Christ
in the eschatological sense, he saw him as the embodiment of
all that was evil.' 'It will have been in this winter (1941) that
Bonhoeffer expressed himself as willing to take part in an
attempt on Hitler's life, if this were required of him.'[12]

Bonhoeffer was already in prison by the time of the events of July 1944, though he would pay the ultimate price for the failure of the assassination attempt. By that year, a widespread conspiracy existed in Germany, composed of army officers, lawyers, intellectuals, some from the old German aristocracy, and churchmen, who were determined to deliver their country from Hitler's power.

A key figure in the bomb-plot was Colonel Count Claus von Stauffenberg, supported by his brother Berthold. It was Claus who planted and primed the bomb at a military briefing in Hitler's headquarters at Rastenburg. At the last moment, the bomb, secreted in a briefcase, was moved from an open position close to Hitler, to rest under a heavy oak map table, which successfully deflected the blast. The hot afternoon meant that windows were open and the force of the bomb dissipated.

The Stauffenberg brothers were devout Roman Catholics. In H. H. Kirst's *The 20th of July* there is a moving account of the brothers' movements in Berlin on 19 July. At about 8.00 pm the brothers meet at a military headquarters and set off in Claus' car. 'At Dahlem, on the way to the Wannsee, they passed a church. Evensong was in progress, and the sound of organ music drifted out into the street through open doors. Claus told his driver to stop. For a moment he seemed to hesitate before entering the church. Then, squaring his shoulders, he strode inside. He stood at the back of the nave for some minutes, still and motionless, with his head bowed in silent prayer. He did not speak again until they reached their destination.' [13]

Here was a prayer for delivery backed by the faithfulness and commitment of very many deeply troubled and anxious men and women, whose very lives were at stake, and whose Christianity had led them to a dangerous course of action. But this proved to be an occasion when the battle was not the Lord's. Indeed the bloodbath which followed the events of 20 July 1944 swept away the Stauffenbergs, Dietrich Bonhoeffer, and hundreds with them.

What contour of God can be made in the complexity of

intercession for delivery, which will seem sometimes to have been given and sometimes to have been withheld? Many will have stories of delivery and escape. Others, like the conspirators of 1944, will have found a different tale told. Doubtless there will even be claims by religious people that God fights on their side. Yet it would be a reduction of his nature to believe, as the author of the books of Samuel believed, that God's power of delivery can be commanded or intercepted in battle.

The accurate contours of a God who delivers may lie in the extraordinary efficacy of a detailed and renewable relationship with divine involvement in the ups and downs, the dangers and the fears of the life of every individual. The reality of a deepened prayer life is the reality of the constant observation of response. For so many faithful people, in conditions of extreme anxiety, it can seem indeed that 'the battle is the Lord's ... and that the Lord saves not with sword and spear'.[14]

Faithfulness in prayer life sows a harvest of both immediate and ongoing productivity. In the perspective of today's modern Germany and modern Europe, who can say where the prayers and faithfulness of Dietrich Bonhoeffer and the Stauffenberg brothers and so many other brave men and women of their generation have contributed? For a God who is involved in everyday history, as the Old Testament writers believed him to be, there is no knowing where delivery now, delivery ahead, and delivery yet to be will make its own remarkable manifestation. Christian people are called not to be exultant decoders of divine involvement in events which they cannot understand. They are called to be faithful in the enterprise of a daily relationship with God's love.

At that watershed moment which the Church calls the Ascension, when the Holy Spirit became the gift of the Risen Christ to the Church which was about to be born, St Luke records events thus:

> 'So when they had come together, they asked him: "Lord, will you at this time restore the kingdom to

Israel?" He said to them: "It is not for you to know times or seasons which the Father has fixed by his own authority". But you shall receive power when the Holy Spirit has come upon you.'[15]

Chapter 8

The Resourcing God:

Solomon's Dream

(1 Kings 3. 4–15)

DREAMS ARE a mixed kaleidoscope of experience. Sometimes, they seem to be a bizarre cocktail of weird fantasies. Sometimes, a dream becomes a nightmare, often with repeated, frightening ingredients: trees falling on the dreamer, imprisonment in closed spaces, trains which cannot be caught, cars which crash. Sometimes dreams are reassuring and gentle. Waking from such a dream can be startingly uncomfortable, when new securities, visions of placid beauty and of a new and reassuring life fade with day-break. Those who have died often appear in dreams and their voices can be very clear. Dreams tell us something of our own moods, of our longings, of our insecurities, of our hopes and fears, of our loves and hates.

Solomon's encounter with God at Gibeon comes in the form of a dream in which he enters into a dialogue. Solomon's ascent of the throne about the year 960 BC had brought its own sense of challenge and uncertainty. The Israelite tribes had become welded into a new sense of solidarity under the charisma and military and political skills of King David. A new era of settled nationhood had begun, with security of borders, an established capital at Jerusalem, and a centralised administration vested in the monarchy. Even so, the last days of David's reign had been beset by rebellion and rivalry culminating in the revolt of Absalom. Solomon's own ascent to the throne had been accomplished only at the price of the murder of his older half-brother, Adonijah. There is uncertainty about the legality of his actions, and the moral nature of the accession, which had rested only on the verbal promise of the failing David. The history is given us by an historian probably of Josiah's reign, about 620 BC, who is at pains to explain the story of the succession of disasters which appears to him to have beset the tribes since the Golden Age of David's rule, three hundred years before. This writer's perspective is one of religious and cultic purity, and he sees the preceding history as a history of religious failure, of syncretism with local gods, of the personal failure of a succession of kings and rulers. In the view of the Deuteronomic historian of the books of Kings, Solomon, for all his bright start, began the rot.

None the less, in the early years, there are signs of promise. Indeed the history of Solomon's reign seems to have been alight with the diplomatic skills of local alliances, through marriage to the King of Egypt's daughter, through friendship with the Phoenician dynasty headed by the powerful King Hiram of Tyre, through royal visits, notably by the Queen of Sheba. The kingdom was rich in resources and blessed by peaceful co-existence with neighbouring tribes. Solomon's reign would see the building of the temple in all its glory. At the beginning all looks fair. Later would come political and financial corruption, an obsession with an ever-widening harem of women and, worst of all in the eyes of the historian, the worship of other gods, as influenced by Solomon's many foreign concubines.

In the salad days of Solomon's reign, his encounter with God at Gibeon has a richness of its own. In the context of the dream, all the vulnerability and uncertainty of Solomon's character is revealed. Often, in the depths of our unconscious, the real person, the real motive, the real hope becomes clarified in a dream. We are wise if we watch our dreams and try to decipher what they are telling us.

Solomon is realistic about his situation. He is aware of the success and skills of his father. Presumably he is only too aware of the methods which he has used to ensure his succession. He declares his inexperience and incompetence, his sense of inadequacy and need for guidance. In his dream, Solomon prays for the gift of discernment. In the story of the encounter Solomon is promised that gift of wisdom, and because he has asked for such a morally appropriate gift, he is promised in addition riches and honour, conditional on his moral and religious conduct, with that great desire of the ancient world, long life. What does the story of Solomon's dream tell us about the contours of God?

First, God is encountered in the depth and ground of our being. It is in the setting of a dream that Solomon is able to present to God the reality of his own sense of fear and inability. So much of our prayer life can become a way of seeking to fool ourselves in our relationship with God. It is easy to make our approach to the God who is waiting for us, masked in a disguise of our own construction. In the clarity of his dream Solomon is able to present himself as vulnerable and able to admit it; as threatened by the successes and achievements of his father.

Much of the worshipping life of the modern Church pays scant heed to the importance of self-examination and confession. For all sorts of good reasons, we have sought to break away from the heavy sense of guilt and unworthiness which was part of the legacy of the 16th century Reformers. It is only too easy for Christian life and witness to build its sense of the acceptance by God of us, for all that we think we are, without facing the certainty that God meets us where we actually are, not where we would like to be. We fail to see that he meets us in all the muddle of our motives, of our real desires, of our disappointments and our expectations.

From what we know of Solomon and his character, it was uncharacteristic of him to present himself at Gibeon in this naked and exposed way. There was much in Solomon that was lustful, greedy, ambitious, violent and unprincipled. Indeed, later there will be another encounter with God at Gibeon, once the temple has become complete, and the danger before Solomon of false worship and moral turpitude will be clearly explained.[1] In the context of the story as it is told to us, a window of opportunity is offered to Solomon because, in the exposure of the dream experience, a part of Solomon is able to respond to the offer which God makes. Lurking beneath the surface are all sorts of shadows and fantasies. In reality, his longing for wealth and power and popularity are probably as real a part of him as his sense of need for wisdom. In the encounter with God, his mask is stripped from him. He must face himself and he must face the God whom he encounters.

God meets us at the point in us where we are open and naked. When that happens, it is likely that the encounter becomes full of energy. Our unmasking is part of our Christian search. We need the courage and resolution to look hard at ourselves and to entrust that process to the God who calls us. He meets us very often at the very point when we have been broken down by a sense of loss or failure or loss of confidence or missed direction. At these points so common to human experience, God invites us as he invited Solomon: 'Ask what I shall give you'.[2] There is a sense in which God will give us that for which we ask.

It is so often part of our affliction that we think we know what we want, but when we have received it, it was never what we thought we wanted. Part of our faith-journey is one of exploration in which we explore our motives, our hopes, our desires. It is important to remember that God will meet us in that ground of our being, in the depth of who we really are and of what we think we really want.

Alessandro Pronzato in his book Meditations on the Sand uses his experience of contemplation in the Sahara desert to unfold some of the riches of the spiritual life. He writes: 'The man in the market place may be well-informed, but he suffers from amnesia. He may be abreast of current events, but if he tries to recall what happened yesterday his memory breaks down. He may know where he is, but he has no idea where he comes from and where he is going ... It is only in the desert that you can recall what you ought to be. In the market place you are a number, and the computer can count you. In the desert you discover your true name'.[3] And: 'Prayer is an exploration of the unknown depths of your being. And it could yield a few surprising finds. In the desert you could walk until the soles of your feet are completely worn off; yet, in a spiritual sense, you become a man of the desert only when you journey into the depths of your inner self. Then boredom gives way to surprise after surprise ...'[4]

And Kahlil Gibran in The Prophet writes: 'And if you but listen in the stillness of the night you shall hear them saying in silence: "Our God, who art our winged self, it is thy will in us that willeth. It is thy desire in us that desireth. It is thy urge in us that would turn our nights, which are thine, into days, which are thine also. We cannot ask thee for aught, for thou knowest our needs before they are born in us: Thou art our need; and in giving us more of thyself thou givest us all".' [5]

It is part of the contours of God to lead us into an encounter with him where the truth of ourselves will become more clear and more distilled. Here the reality of our desires and hopes, our longings and our wants can be open to the healing strength of the God who knows us and wills to use us in his service and for the establishment of his rule on earth.

So it is that, opened up, as it were, to both his vulnerability and his real aspiration for wealth and identity, Solomon asks for the gift of discernment and wisdom. This contour of God is both resourcing and enriching.

The 1662 Prayer Book has an abundance of collects which speak of the human need for discernment and of God's will to resource that need:

Epiphany 1: '... grant that they may both perceive and know what things they ought to do, and also may have grace and power faithfully to fulfil the same ...'

Easter 4: '... that they may love the thing which thou commandest and desire that which thou dost promise ...'

Easter 5: 'Grant ... that by thy holy inspiration we may think those things that be good ...'

Whitsun: 'Grant us by the same Spirit to have a right judgement in all things.'

Trinity 9: 'Grant to us, Lord, we beseech thee, the spirit to think and do always such things as be rightful'.

Trinity 10: 'Let thy merciful ears, O Lord, be open to the prayers of thy humble servants; and that they may obtain their petitions make them to ask such things as shall please thee ...'

Trinity 14: '... Mercifully grant that thy Holy Spirit may in all things direct and rule our hearts.'[6]

The wealth of spirituality in the prayer book collects present an image of recognition that because God answers our prayers and resources our requests, it is crucial for us to develop our motivation and desires so that they can harmonise with the direction of God's goodness and lovingkindness.

At the beginning of his reign, Solomon offers his need for the gift of discernment and soon after the story of the dream, we are given an example of the new king's wisdom, in the event of the two prostitutes or inn-keepers, one of whom steals a baby from another, and who ask for judgement. However, in the eyes of the historian who wrote the book of Kings, Solomon's early promise is not maintained.

It is part of the nature of God to give to us what we ask. If it is of his way to give us gifts and resources, powers and skills, talents and abilities, it must be part of our response to that way to seek to build up our own discernment of how we should use what we are given and of how we should handle our real needs and wants.

Both Matthew and Luke describe Jesus' celebrated parable of the talents in two different ways. (Matthew 25. 14–30) and (Luke 19. 11–27). In both stories it seems clear that the teaching disclosed is one of the generosity and truthfulness of God, the variation in resource and ability experienced by people, and the essential nature of risk-taking and endeavour in the service of the Kingdom of God.

The contours of God presented in the story of Solomon's dream at Gibeon is one of generosity and out-pouring love. Not only will the gift of discernment be granted, but riches and blessings of many kinds will be given as well. The character of Solomon's response has its own mix of variableness and uncertainty. At one level, he is unconfident and uncertain; at another he desires much for himself. In the story of Solomon's use of the gifts he is given, his own equivocation and sense of personal success become his own undoing. He grows into a risk-taker, but the risks he takes are founded in a desire for personal aggrandisement, when the real risk which he should be facing is the risk of exposing his true nature to himself before God.

Jesus said: 'Take heed what you hear, the measure you give will be the measure you get, and still more will be given you. For to him who has more will be given; and from him who has not, even what he has will be taken away'.[7]

There is a law both of appreciating and diminishing returns. The tragedy of Solomon was to have begun with appreciation and to have ended with diminishment. It is an easy tragedy to befall. So rich is the resourcing of God that we are wise to ask for what we really want and not for what we think we want, and to seek to be aware of the difference.

'Almighty and everlasting God, who art always more ready to hear than we to pray, and art wont to give more than we either desire or deserve; Pour down upon us the abundance of thy mercy; forgiving us those things whereof our conscience is afraid, and giving us those good things which we are not worthy to ask, but through the merits and mediation of Jesus Christ, thy Son, Our Lord.'[8] (Collect for Trinity 12)

Chapter 9

The God Who Finds Us:
Elijah meets God on Mount Horeb
(1 Kings 19. 9–18)

THE SETTING to Elijah's encounter in a cave on the 'mountain of God', where Moses had received his commission, is one of political and religious turmoil. Following the death of Solomon, the kingdom has become divided, and the Deuteronomic historian describing, some two hundred years later, the events of the 9th century BC is judgemental on many of the personalities of the day. Their religious compromises, he believes, were responsible for the disorder.

Elijah appears upon the scene of the Northern Kingdom about the year 850 BC. The stories about Elijah are an entity, probably a collection of their own, adapted into the historian's work. Here, in the Northern Kingdom, rules King Ahab, a weak and vacillating character, dominated by his Phoenician wife Jezebel. She is a woman of violent and ruthless ways, determined to proselytise for the worship of Baal, the fertility mother goddess of the region, and extant in her own land of Tyre. Ahab's father, Omri, has built an established and prosperous capital at the hill of Samaria, and has made certain alliances in part with the Syrians, in expectation of the growing might of Assyria to the north, and in recognition of the division of Judah to the south. Like John the Baptist in years to come, Elijah appears in a garment of hair-cloth and a girdle of leather and arrives as an instant challenge to the influence of Jezebel and the religious corruption of the people. Indeed, the historian of the books of Kings sees him as a Moses-like figure restoring a sense of continuity in the religious tradition, being fed by ravens in the wilderness, challenging the cultic observances of the Baals and leading the people backwards and onwards to a recovery of the promised land of historical faith.

It is therefore part of the silhouette of Elijah's ministry that his encounter with God, which will lead to the dénouement

61

of Ahab and Jezebel's reign, should take place at Mount
Horeb in Sinai, where Moses had met God in the burning
bush. Forty days and forty nights, like the journey of the
Israelites in the wilderness, is the symbolic travelling time
which has brought Elijah from Beersheba to Sinai. His journey there into Judah from the north had been precipitated by
fear of Jezebel's vengeance after Elijah's slaughter of the
prophets of Baal at Mount Carmel, despite his prophecy of
rain to end a disastrous drought.

It is at Beersheba that we come across Elijah under a
broom tree apparently experiencing the first waves of a clin-
ical depression: 'It is enough; now, O Lord, take away my
life; for I am no better than my fathers'[1] A combination of
fear, physical exertion, reaction, despair at the perfidy of
human behaviour, and a sense of religious failure, all appear
to have contributed to a feeling of personal worthlessness
and dark depression.

The text tells us that he is fed and sustained in this first
wave of hopelessness. The cake baked on hot stones and the
jar of water, which are awaiting Elijah when he awakes, provide a parallel with the manna and the quails given to the
Israelite tribes at the time of corporate despair at the hunger
of the wilderness. In the strength of this food he is fortified
for the journey to the cave on the Mount of Horeb where the
encounter with God is to take place.

Here, in the cave, comparable to the cleft in the rock where
Moses was allowed to see the back of God, but not the face,
God seeks him out. The first encounter sounds imperious and
threatening: 'What are you doing here, Elijah?'[2] In the confusion of our constant need to try to escape the traumas,
demands, and complexities of our lives, we are sought out by
God and challenged. Our escapes may be metaphorical or
actual. We may literally run from the demands being put
upon us. A vicar appointed to a new and unwelcoming
parish, faced with what looked like initially impossible
demands, simply left after twentyfour hours and had to be
found in the isolation of a holiday cottage and coaxed back
into the new parish. Sometimes our sense of escape may be

much less obvious. People who sit outside a circle, who
manoeuvre their chairs to face backwards to others, who
stand apart in conversations, who walk behind others, may
be battling with their own call to escape. Sometimes our
inclination to escape takes us back to places where we have
felt a sense of previous security or value. Escapers will visit
places where they were once known or where they contributed. Elijah's escape to the Mount of Horeb makes its
own statement about the past, about longing, about the loss
of security.

One of the most powerful poems which expresses the
human longing for escape is in William Butler Yeats' poem:
The Lake Isle of Innisfree:

> I will arise and go now, and go to Innisfree,
> And a small cabin build there, of clay and wattles made;
> Nine bean rows will I have there, a hive for the honey-
> bee,
> And live alone in the bee-loud glade.
> And I shall have some peace there, for peace comes
> dropping slow,
> Dropping from the veils of the morning to where the
> cricket sings;
> There midnight's all a-glimmer, and noon a purple glow,
> And evening full of the linnet's wings.
>
> I will arise and go now, for always night and day
> I hear lake water lapping with low sounds by the shore;
> While I stand on the roadway, or on the pavement gray,
> I hear it in the deep heart's core.[3]

In his isolation and loneliness, Elijah is confronted by the
reality of God's claims. The encounter presents us with a contour of God which appears challenging and inescapable.
Elijah should be at the heart of his ministry. He should be
engaging with the cut and thrust of his challenge to the apostasy of the people. He should be facing up to the dangerous,
mercurial nature of Jezebel and her threats.

Or should he? Is this aspect of God not the shape of the

school master who has found the schoolboy smoking behind the bicycle shed? Is it not our response that will read into the question a sense of guilt and challenge? Is it not our reflection that wants to identify with a 'hardening of the oughteries' in the words of Dr Lake.

Perhaps the question to Elijah is one much more of the reality of God's constant searching claims upon us. Perhaps the question is a reflection of that whole dimension to God which is literally inescapable and which will find us in the reality of our every hiding place.

The psalmist in psalm 139 ascribes to God an all-encompassing shadow and shield. There is nowhere to hide from God. There is nowhere that God will not search one out and 'encompass one behind and before'.

> 'Where shall I go from your spirit:
> or where shall I flee from your presence?
> If I ascend into heaven you are there:
> If I make my bed in the grave you are there also.
> If I spread out my wings towards the morning:
> Or dwell in the uttermost parts of the sea,
> Even there your hand shall lead me:
> And your right hand shall hold me.'[4]

God's nature is one of an insatiable, relentless, unstoppable quest. He searches out his created world and involves himself in the minutiae of all that is. Something of his searching longing is expressed in the words of Our Lord from the cross: 'I thirst'. Here is epitomised for evermore, the longing of God for the souls of all.

'What are you doing here, Elijah?' could be interpreted as the demand of authority, the regulation of a law-maker, or as the involvement of the Creator in the very stuff of the life of one of his created beings. An escaper, hidden in the cave of the ground, isolated, depressed, Elijah is sought by the enticement of the living God.

The cave itself is a symbol of involvement. For Elijah it is a place of illusory safety. At the Incarnation, it will be into the shepherd's cave in the depth of the ground, detached from the community life of Bethlehem, that the Lord will be born. Into the heart of his world comes the Saviour for whom there is no place of safety, no place of welcome, no place of security, but instead the cave-like dwelling inhabited by animals and their keepers. The isolated searching out of Elijah in his cave prefigures this depth of involvement by God in his world. As in the scene at the Bethlehem 'stable', Elijah is a fugitive at the hands of a reckless and indiscriminate authority. He is homeless and insecure. He is far from roots and with no room at an inn. In this isolation he is found by God and the encounter leads to healing and recovery. 'I have been very jealous for the Lord the God of hosts ...'[5]

Elijah's sorrow and depression are poured out. He has been jealous or zealous for the ancient faith of his people. He has tried to maintain his integrity and his sense of vision. He has tried to remain faithful. He has tried to be loyal and steadfast and to maintain the truth of his spirituality. He has struggled in the face of real and imagined abuse, in the face of moral and actual pressure, in the face of a society whose support for its ancient roots and tradition has crumbled away. All Elijah's sense of isolation in his lone crusade for faithfulness and consistency is expressed: 'I even I only am left and they seek my life to destroy it'.[6]

The Christian story is full of isolated and lonely people seeking to maintain an integrity of vision in the face of spiritual and moral collapse. For many in today's climate, a Christian allegiance involves a loneliness and an isolation that may be both emotionally threatening and full of temptation. Elijah stands ahead for all such people, as he laments before the God who has searched him out and found him, the full depth of his depression and his despair.

There is truly a sense in which for many despair will shadow faith. Many human beings are subject to varying degrees of depression. People with a religious persuasion will tend to be people with their own sense of personal expectation. Spiritual and other moral goals will be set, and again and again the targets will be missed. High expectations abound. The more competitive a society becomes, the more prevalent are the aspirations to succeed. The higher the possible summit of achievement is perceived, the more frequent will be the relegation to the foothills. It is not surprising that depression and suicide risk are high amongst university students. Conditions of high unemployment will spawn the incidence of depressive illness. The world of work has for long provided a sense of self-worth and esteem which, once removed, leaves the redundant, and those who have never worked, aimless, depressed, and without confidence, even if rewarded financially for the loss of role.

Depression is no respecter of persons. Its dark tentacles can weave their frightening clasp across every socio-economic group. It can lock itself into the heart of the able and talented, and the low achiever, with equal tenacity. Its incidence is fed by high expectation, by loss, and by a sense of failure. Its characteristics are a loss of personal self-esteem and of confidence and of a sense of hope, and the invasion of dark and sombre feelings of inadequacy. It often attacks the sensitive and aware. It brings with it, at its worst, a fearful internal pain and physical suffering as well as the pain of guilt and a sense of despair.

Elijah exhibits all the symptoms. He has believed himself capable of challenging the apostasy of the priests of Baal. His challenge at Mount Carmel has been outwardly successful, but that success has failed to alter the religious apostasy of the people. He believes himself to be responsible for this failure. He has lost his liberty under the threats of Jezebel. He feels isolated, lonely and despairing.

Typical of many a depressive condition, one can believe that his faith and sense of purpose has been challenged by the débacle of his escape through Judah to Sinai. The shadow side of his faith is paralleled by a sense of inner challenge: is God real in the despair of the present moment? One of the most frightening aspects of depression for a person of faith is the experience of isolation from God. In the depths of the darkness which is so overwhelming, God seems distant, irrelevant and hidden. His very existence seems elusive and uncertain.

Elijah, in the brokenness and despair of his condition, is given an experience of God. First there is a wind, one of those sudden desert winds which emerge without warning and send dust devils swirling across the landscape, churning up stones and loosening rocks on the hillside. Then comes an earthquake, presumably of comparatively small proportions, for Elijah's cave appears to be unthreatened. Then comes a fire. All three manifestations in Old Testament terms are seen as symbols of the presence of God, but the text tells us that God was in none of these three. It is in the fourth revelation, the still, small voice, that God is to be found, and which makes Elijah wrap his face in his mantle.

It is the deafening silence of the encounter which opens up the presence of God. How are we to interpret this contour of the God who finds Elijah and meets him? Somewhere in the depth of our being there is a part of us which will respond to the voice of God.Something inside us is able to communicate in a way which is completely valid and assured, and to hear God at his most profound and real. Surprisingly, this capacity to respond may be at its most sharp at times of spiritual and emotional vulnerability.

Silence is an essential prerequisite to encouraging that communicating receiver. We need to find ways of being still and detached, of being able to hear silence without any interruptions to break it. Most of us are seekers after noise. We turn the television on when we come in from work, the radio on when we are washing up, the cassette player on when we enter a car. We use the telephone to interrupt silence. We make asinine comments to strangers to break up silence. Anglican Christians tend to fear silence particularly. Before acts of worship, it seems that silence must be held at bay at all costs.

In one of our great cathedrals, before daily evensong, I took my place before the choir entered. All around was muffled and not so muffled discussion. Plans were being made for a coffee date. Would Friday at 11.00 am be convenient? Would Nescafé do? Arrangements were being made for cover at a charity shop. Would it be possible to do three hours instead of two? The merits of two competing hairdressers were being compared. The new one that had just opened was undoubtedly the better value.

I went to a funeral in a country church in Suffolk. It was a particularly sad and sudden funeral of someone who had died in their prime. Many were gathering from all sorts of distances. The organist was late. At the back, a churchwarden was in animated discussion with another. In this case, the talk was loud but not so loud as to be able to distinguish the words, simply a discordant and totally inappropriate heavy murmur.

At many churches, before the early service, as worshippers gather in the quiet of the morning, there is a steady sound of cheery welcome, inconsequential pleasantries, the passing of the time of day. Silence appears to be feared before the introduction of the liturgy breaks it up.

In truth, it is in our silence that we will meet God. There is a need for us to cultivate silence in our communities. Corporate silence has a particular power of its own, as has been well known and experienced by the Society of Friends. The still, small voice of Elijah could be that sense of total stillness and total attention which we achieve only rarely, when we have allowed ourselves to become totally undistracted and still, when we have waited on God and found him.

There is a story told of Archbishop Ramsey being interviewed by a radio programme on prayer. He was asked for how long had he prayed that morning. In his inimitable and hesitant manner of speech he replied: 'Well ... I think I prayed ... I prayed for ... about two minutes'. When the interviewer expressed obvious surprise that an Archbishop should have prayed for so short a time, he replied to the effect that it had taken him at least an hour to reach his point of prayer.

Archbishop Bloom tells the story in School for Prayer of an old lady who had been praying for fourteen years but felt that she had never had any sense of God's presence. 'If you speak all the time, you don't give God a chance to place a

THE GOD WHO FINDS US   69

word in'; he told her. The Archbishop, then a young priest, told her to go and sit apart for fifteen minutes a day and knit before the face of God. In due course she came back full of the extraordinary result: 'I felt so quiet because the room was so peaceful. There was a clock ticking but it did not disturb the silence, its ticking just underlined the fact that everything was so still ... I perceived that this silence was not simply an absence of noise, but that the silence had substance. It was not absence of something but presence of something. The silence had a density, a richness, and it began to pervade me. The silence around began to come and meet the silence in me ... All of a sudden I perceived that the silence was a presence. At the heart of the silence there was Him who is all stillness, all peace, all poise.'[7]

The power of silence, when we can find it, is the avenue which opens up for us the chance to encounter the stillness of God. Sometimes moments of great depression, personal loss, a sense of our own breakage can be moments when the still small voice of God contacts the depth of our being and triggers a new sense of his personal and individual concern for us in our need.

For Elijah the encounter is absolute and cathartic. Again he is asked why he is there. Again he presents the lament of his personal isolation. From this encounter he appears to receive a new sense of courage, direction and purpose. Although the command to Elijah to reorder the political balance of power and to slay the prophets of Baal seems to us to be high-handed and violent, in the context of the story, it offers Elijah an opportunity for recovery from the suffering of his lostness and isolation. The contour of God is one of infinite involvement in our lives and one of capacity to communicate with us in the very depth of our despairs.

Kahlil Gibran in *The Prophet* writes: 'There are those among you who seek the talkative through fear of being alone. The silence of aloneness reveals to their eyes their naked selves and they would escape. And there are those who talk, and without knowledge or forethought reveal a truth which they themselves do not understand. And there are those who have the truth within them, but they tell it not in words. In the bosom of such as these the spirit dwells in rhythmic silence.'[8]

In Revelation 34, Julian discloses her experience of the two 'great secrets' of the nature of God. The first is a sense of the profundity of God's involvement in all that is about; the second is the conviction that all is well. The first secret is described thus:

> He *is* Holy Church
> He is the foundation,
> He is the essence,
> He is the teaching,
> He is the teacher,
> He is the goal,
> He is the reward for which every natural soul toils.[9]

And Jesus said to them: 'Come away by yourselves to a lonely place, and rest awhile', for many were coming and going and they had no leisure even to eat. And they went away in the boat to a lonely place by themselves.[10]

Chapter 10

The Holiness of God:

The Vision of Isaiah of Jerusalem

(Isaiah 6. 1–8)

ISAIAH GIVES a clear date for his encounter with the holiness of God: 742 BC, the year in which King Uzziah died. In fact the prophecy is written probably at a later date, perhaps near the turn of the 7th century when the Judah of Uzziah's prosperous reign has become severely threatened by the aggrandisement of Assyria and the invasion of the Northern Kingdom. It is a time of turmoil and danger, and Isaiah is reflecting on the origins of his faith and contemplating the nature of his contemporary world. Some of his reflections may be taking account of what he sees as his own sense of failure to propagate a prophetic message which will be heard, and thus lead to a change of religious heart and hence to a change in political security.

It would seem probable that Isaiah was a citizen of Jerusalem, a town dweller. The period of all his prophecies covered some forty years, and he would have seen change after change on the political map, including the fall of Samaria in 721 BC and the invasion of Palestine in 701 under Sennacherib. It is possible that Isaiah came from a well-to-do educated class in the city. He seems to have been married to a 'prophetess'. Much of his teaching concerns the promise of the recovery of the true king-ship of God in a future 'day of the Lord'. Then there will be a reversal of all the misfortunes and incompetencies of the day, and a new vision of peace and order and mutual solidarity will replace the religious and political muddle.

Within the prophetic thinking lies a perception of God as the 'King enthroned' whose sense of judgement and righteousness will determine the cause of history. Isaiah calls the people to enthrone God in their hearts anew in a message with which our contemporary faith can easily identify. Part of his vision encompasses a new age, part political and part

spiritual, in which a new king will reign. So begins the
Messianic vision picked up so movingly in Isaiah 11 which
helps to prepare religious perception for the coming of Our
Lord, and may sow some seeds of interpretation ahead of
Jesus' teaching about the Kingdom of God.

Isaiah's reflection on his call to prophecy may be coloured
by his own sense of inadequacy at his failure to fulfil his ministry effectively. He appears to be bewildered by the peoples'
dullness and blindness. The context of his call may be
coloured by the later experience of his response. None the
less, his experience of God has an authenticity about it which
leaves a deep impression and appears overwhelming. Here is
the story of a man of faith encountering God in all the reality of his numinous presence. Here is described a deep recognition of a summons to service, a response from an
experience that spoke of God's individual call. This call challenged, with its holiness, the human character of Isaiah's
faith.

It is in Solomon's temple that the holiness of God is
revealed. It is probable that Isaiah is to be found in the courtyard of the temple looking up the steps past the two external
pillars known as Jachin and Boaz, gazing through into the
sanctuary beyond the table of the show-bread and the altar
of incense. Through the smoke from this last, he would have
seen dimly the steps leading up to the Holy of Holies. Here,
he would have known, rested the ark of the covenant of God
and he would have believed that in the cedar-panelled room,
a perfect cube, guarded by the two golden cherubim with
their extended wings, dwelt the presence of God, living
among his people.

Isaiah is clear that his vision constituted a direct meeting
with God. He remembers quite clearly the year in which the
encounter befell. His testimony is that 'he saw the Lord, sitting upon a throne, high and lifted up'.[1] The vision includes
mystical accompaniments: seraphim, – mysterious, visionary,
angel-like figures – are part of the picture surrounding God.
There is movement and a sense of obeisance. The seraphim
are worshipping and calling. The refrain of the Sanctus, the

Holiness of God, is a constant feature of their presentation. The smoke from the incense fills the temple, and so profound is the vision that it seems as if the very foundations of the great building are shaking at the presence of God. Psalm 18 verse 8 speaks the same language: 'The earth heaved and quaked, the foundations of the hills were shaken'.[2]

Isaiah's reaction is to feel an immediate sense of inadequacy and personal failure. So profound is the reality of God's majesty and being that he feels distanced and ashamed, both for himself and for the people with whom he associates solidarity and responsibility. So deep does the trance of spiritual engagement become that he sees one of the seraphim coming with a live coal from the altar of incense to purge his guilt. With that purging is born a sense of vocation and self-worth, even if the immediate message from that commission appears to be obscurely uncompromising and unforgiving. At the heart of the vision lies a sense of personal one-to-one relationship with God, in which choice, value and renewal are part of the vocational experience.

There is an extraordinary veracity about the story of Isaiah's call which reaches us down the centuries, and which cuts through the more unusual cultic frills to the recorded experience. At the heart of the encounter seems to lie a recognition of the holiness or 'otherness' of God which yet bridges any gap that may exist between God and man and which reaches the core of Isaiah's soul. God is both holy and knowable. The meeting with him is both overwhelming and personal. God is both awe-ful and yet approachable. The contour of God for Isaiah is indeed a contour of holiness, but that holiness is not a barrier but a means of drawing and including.

Isaiah uses picture language to speak of the holiness of God. God's very holiness is in itself a distancing force, just because human beings cannot speak authentically of holiness. It is a definition which is by its very concept beyond us. God alone is holy, and our knowledge of holiness is as limited as our knowledge of God. Even when God is in some measure known, that knowledge is partial and weak.

Holiness only becomes perceptible to us at the imperfect level at which we can come to know God. We are like blind people groping in a tunnel of darkness enabled only by pin-pricks of distant light, which can lead us towards some greater illumination. The existence of the pin-pricks alone encourages and enables us. We are drawn and upheld by them. The more we move toward them, the more valid they become, but our knowledge is restricted by the confines of our tunnel.

The good news of the Christian Gospel is of course the great affirmation that into the darkness of our restricted vision has come the holiness of God, to be seen in the face of Jesus Christ. The gap has been bridged. The darkness has been illuminated. The unknowable has become known. The truth has been revealed. The light has shone in the darkness and the darkness has never overcome it.

In the later 20th century there is an acceleration of change of every kind. New ways are needed of perceiving the nature of God in the complexity of a changing cultural and socio-logical order. The task of the Christian Church is to interpret the face of God to each generation. The God who is involved in his world, who is deeply part of the process of growth and evolution, will present many and various facets of himself. In the search for the new face of God, it is possible to lose sight of that old face of which the holiness, seen by Isaiah, is such a feature. I once heard a preacher, criticising new perceptions of an understanding of God, declare that in place of the roar-ing lion of the glory of God we had tried to substitute a tame pussy cat.

The holiness of God glimpsed by Isaiah was a face which spoke of otherness and of something beyond human com-prehension. The search for God will lead us into the possi-bility of finding him in his holiness and thus in a remoteness. The encounter will bring with it an experience of both the distance and the nearness of God's presence. Isaiah described a sense both of something beyond himself and of something which comes close to him, and which relates directly and per-sonally. His vision of God brings God close, and yet the vision itself is unsettling, daunting and full of personal challenge.

How are Christians today to encounter something of the holiness of God? What will speak of that otherness of God's nature which is both distant and near-to?

First of all, it was in the context of worship that Isaiah saw the Lord high and lifted up. The enormous value of buildings and places must never be lost. It is right that people should make pilgrimages and journeys to places of particular historical holiness, so that they may kneel where, in the words of T S Eliot's *Four Quartets* on Little Gidding, prayer has been valid.[3] There is a statement about travel to a place of worship and sanctity that can speak of the search for encounter. It is in the nature of such a journey that, on arrival, one may savour and imbibe a place and an atmosphere which it has been costly in time and money and energy to find. Again, T S Eliot's Journey of the Magi speaks of the nature of discovery at the end of an arduous expedition to find one facet of God, only to be shown another.

'A cold coming we had of it,
Just the worst time of the year
For a journey, and such a long journey:
The ways deep and the weather sharp,
The very dead of winter

...

All this was a long time ago, I remember,
And I would do it again, but set down
This set down
This: were we led all that way for
Birth or Death? There was a Birth, certainly,
We had evidence and no doubt. I had seen birth and
        death,
But had thought they were different; this Birth was
Hard and bitter agony for us, like Death, our death,
We returned to our places, these Kingdoms,

But no longer at ease here, in the old dispensation,
With an alien people clutching their gods.
I should be glad of another death.'[4]

It may be at one of the great centres of pilgrimage and
prayerfulness, either at home or abroad, that something of
God's holiness may be revealed. It may be in a place much
more off the beaten track, in some tiny country church, or in
the chapel or undercroft of an urban church, that God is
found. God's holiness is everywhere but it was in the temple
that Isaiah found it. That is why buildings and places can aid
us in our search.

The organised worship of the Church too, should speak of
God's holiness, of his otherness and yet of his closeness.
Isaiah's experience took place in the context of worship. So
often worship becomes a synthesis of mixed human signals
where liturgy and tradition and personal taste all become
confused in a mix of local aspiration. An example of this was
given to me at a service at an Episcopal church in Scotland.
It was a large church and the congregation was small. As so
often, the congregation scattered itself distantly around the
large building, immediately losing any sense of the cohesion
of God's love for all who call on his name. No one took care
to show a stranger where to sit. I went to the front, in order
to seek to affirm something of an approach to God, and sat
in a pew which, at the end of the service, I noticed carried a
card: 'The Episcopal Church of Scotland welcomes you. The
... family has worshipped in this pew since 1888'.

Who was welcoming whom? How crucially must congregations learn to incorporate the stranger and the new-comer!
How crucially must worship become accessible to those
unfamiliar with local customs and traditions!

I was told by an ordained minister who had left the ministry of the Church whilst working in secular employment,
and who was not exercising any official ministry, of the experience of visiting a London church. Half-way through the
Communion service, the scattered congregation moved forward to gather round the altar for the consecration. At the

given moment, everyone moved, but no one related to anyone else. My friend followed along failing to realise that she needed to bring a hymn and prayer book with her, and no one thought to tell her. The experience was one of exclusion and distance. What is going on here belongs to someone else and does not need or want me.

How important it is for Christian communities to work at liturgy and worship so that it can speak both of the holiness of God and of the accessibility of God! It is a hard middle way which preserves the sanctity and richness of worship, and yet includes the disparate community in the access route to its God. This middle way is wary of the 'club church' local in-group with all its matey sense of belonging. It shows an inclusive openness to all who come and a validation of people as people are. It seeks a balance between a structure of worship which is accessible at the lowest common denominator and the preservation of beauty in language and symbol which will enhance and touch the spirit of encounter deep in human hearts.

Isaiah found God in his holiness in the context of the worship of the temple. There are many ways of encountering the holiness of God and organised religious worship is by no means the only one. It is simply that the text does tell us that Isaiah's call began with an experience of worship. This textual revelation demands of worshipping communities an incentive to plan their worshipping in order to facilitate the possibility of meeting the holiness of God. That, and no other, should be the cardinal motivation.

So often worship seems to be structured to take account of very many other considerations. Different styles and orders, traditions and methods become rallying points for attracting the peccadilloes of the religious mind. People will pack round a symbol, be it guitars, or matins, or incense, or the 1662 Prayer Book, or charismatic songs, and rally to that standard of personal experience as a talisman of its own and as if this was the only way to God. There are all sorts of diverse ways of worshipping the holiness of God and different traditions and patterns find their own adherents and methods of deepening faith. What always needs to be held up as a crucial aim is the recognition of the holiness of God and that our worship, whatever tradition or usage may be our custom, has, as its only purpose, the glorification of God's holy name, and not the preservation of the mores of a tribal club.

Dom Gregory Dix, at the conclusion of *The Shape of the Liturgy* recounts of the Eucharist all the diverse happenings and experiences of human circumstance, in which the only fitting response has been to break the bread in remembrance. At the end of his catalogue of differing and varying occasions and emotions and thanksgivings, he writes: 'And best of all, week by week and month by month, on a hundred thousand successive Sundays, faithfully and unfailingly, across all the parishes of Christendom, the pastors have done this just to make the plebs sancta Dei ... the holy common people of God'. [5] Here is the ultimate in the structure of worship: the Eucharist in all its enormously varied styles and manners and theologies, used on such a variety of different occasions and needs, offered simply to make holy the common people of God, and in that holiness to reach God's holiness.

One of the main credentials of the Christian Church is the worship of God: the giving of value and worth to the God the Church believes in. It is therefore essential for Christian communities to give high priority and value to the ensuring that worship is holy. Whatever ingredients or methods or styles or traditions are incorporated, the objective must be to assist conditions where the holiness of God can break through upon the worshipper and some glimpse of his otherness and his depth transport human beings from the banality of their daily lives onto the threshold of heaven.

Such was the experience of Isaiah as he waited in the courtyard of Solomon's temple and peered through into the majesty of the sacred building where perhaps the priests were preparing the evening sacrifice. The consequence of the vision, as we read it, was a sense of guilt and unworthiness just because he had seen the King, the Lord of Hosts.

If worship must be designed and modelled to enable an apprehension of the holiness of God, so must the life of the

Christian community be structured to sustain and heal the feelings of remorse and inadequacy which a real vision of God will provoke. All too often, Christian allegiance has been an entry-point into a sense of personal worthlessness and repressed guilt. The Church has seemed to introduce people to a latent sense of morbid guilt by presenting a whole series of prohibitions and requirements. Then, having saddled the persuaded with a problem of low self-esteem and a sense of inadequacy, it has presented its Gospel as the solution to the problem.

In truth the Gospel is the good news of the holiness of God, which breaks into the midst of our humdrum and unsatisfactory lives and calls us into a relationship with the holiness beyond ourselves. In so doing we are accepted and recreated, not for what we have done or failed to do, but simply for who we are. St Paul speaks in 2 Corinthians 5: of 'a new creation; the old has passed away, behold, the new has come. All this is from God who through Christ reconciled us to himself ...'[6] So often, this new creation is very hard to discern in the corporate or individual life of a faith community. Where such a community *has* glimpsed the holiness of God it will be transparent for all to see.

A Church which perceives the holiness of God will also be restoring and renewing the lives of its community. Perhaps it is here that the ministry of encouragement is so crucial. That ministry avoids the temptations of a mutual admiration society but finds in its members a reason for affirmation and a well of gifts. The new creation begins to be glimpsed when people discover in themselves, through the encouragement of others, resources and attributes which they never realised that they possessed. We cannot know how Isaiah came to find his vocation, but we know from his story that his sense of guilt was purged in the vision of worship and in the ministry of the attendant angelic beings. In the encouragement of the experience, he responded to the call to service and renewal.

An act of worship which includes the ministry of healing has its own particular way of offering windows onto the holiness of God. Here opportunities for innovative and unstructured worship can be explored in a necessarily more corporate way than is always easy for liturgy-based churches. Particular themes, symbols, music, candles, can be employed in a way that breaks out of the Sunday by Sunday mould, important as that still is for discovering the holiness of God. Such an offering, whether it involves anointing, or laying on of hands, or counselling, or prayer, or a combination of all, affirms by its very structure the wholeness and healing which touched Isaiah in the symbol of a burning coal. The preparation for such a service can in itself incorporate others into a perception of the holiness of God and the call of God to wholeness and service.

It is important too for church buildings to develop a corner where an attempt to invite the holiness of God is specifically made and in a more concentrated way than will be possible in the wider building. I once attended, a course for clergy entitled 'The parish priest and prayer'. The leader of the course had travelled widely in Rumania and, with the use of coloured transparencies, he explained how the old monasteries of Rumania had acted as sanctuaries for the local community. Round the outside would be a wall, and near the heart of the complex would be the church. Inside this would be a place of special devotion, a chapel complete with carpets and cushions, and ikons and lights, and a samovar with hot tea, awaiting the faithful to restore themselves in body and spirit in the presence of the holiness of God, and in the comfortable security of his presence. It was from that Eastern European method that I determined to develop a chapel, in the parish church which I served, as a place of beauty and peace where the ambience of holiness could be glimpsed, enabled by statues, ikons, a carpet, embroidery, lighting. The scheme came to fruition only at the cost of vociferous opposition, based on the grounds of cost and style and purpose, even though the parish had a good record on missionary giving and the money was to hand. Once the chapel had been beautifully refurnished, it began to act as something of a magnet for quiet and daily prayer and contemplation and, for some, a vision of the holiness of God.

Many people will have had their own experience which parallels the experience of Isaiah. My own came to me as a young man training in the army for a commission. I can remember the year! the month! It was October. I was sent on a so-called 'battle camp' on the borders of Herefordshire and Wales. One Sunday afternoon, after a week of intense training, I walked in the hills high above the military camp and rapidly became absorbed by the stillness, the silence and the grandeur. High above human habitation, in the wild peacefulness of the Welsh hills, it became possible to feel encountered by the reality of something very much beyond myself. Although I had received a traditional Christian upbringing, it was my first recognition of something deeply other than myself, the holiness and completeness of God.

After a long walk across a moorland track, as the evening sun was setting, I followed the trail down into a small Welsh village. The church bell was ringing and the local community were gathering for Evensong. To my surprise, I found myself drawn into the welcoming light of the church porch as the dusk settled in. Inside, the liturgy was in Welsh, which I did not speak, but the singing was so superb and uplifting that it led me into an early perception that there is a reality about the Divine which had put some kind of claim upon me. I do not remember a feeling of unworthiness, but I do remember a feeling of longing. Here was something deeply 'other' than the ordinariness of daily life as expressed in military service.

That day on the hills and in the worship of that country village, I met the living God, even though my vocation took several more years to mature. The words heard by Isaiah have a power and authority which traverse the centuries. The contour and shape of God is not only holy but deeply personal and distilled into the capacity to relate one to one. 'Whom shall I send and who will go for us?'. Then I said: 'Here am I, send me'.[7]

Chapter 11

The Vocational God:

The Summons of Jeremiah
(Jeremiah 1. 4–10)

MY OWN personal introduction to the book of Jeremiah was my introduction to theology. In almost my first day at Theological College I was set the task of reading the book and writing an essay on what I thought was its message. The new academic year began in early August and it was the holiday season. The sun shone, and outside the library tourists were visiting the cathedral city. Under the shadow of the rising pinnacles, and the great west face, children were playing, lovers reclined on the grass, picnickers spread themselves, pretty girls walked by. Through the windows, an idyllic holiday scene mocked a new student grappling with the message of Jeremiah. Part of me began to hate him. What could this all mean? What relevance had these ancient words, set in what looked like pre-history, to the contemporary world of England in the 1960s? What was the purpose of surrendering two potential careers to exile oneself in the stuffy irrelevance of a theological library, when, outside beckoned a world of sunshine and holiday-making, of exploring and relaxing?

I battled with the complexities of the historical background and the confusing mix of oracles, prophecies and personal testimony. Part of me identified with some of the despair and depression in the prophet's writings. In years since, I have come to value much of the book and to perceive an extraordinary doggedness, valour and faithfulness in many of the passages.

Jeremiah has been the victim of 'labelling' when he has been presented as a prophet of gloom, largely on the grounds of the message in the Book of Lamentations, which it seems unlikely that he wrote. Brewer's Dictionary describes 'a Jeremiah' as a 'pitiful tale, a tale of woe to produce compassion'.[1] Though not often used today, the expression 'a Jeremiah' is employed occasionally to describe a gloomy and pessimistic person. In fact, there is much in the book of Jeremiah which is immensely hopeful and affirmative.

In my early and unhappy introduction to the academic study of 'the faith once delivered to saints', it was to the call of Jeremiah in chapter one, that I returned and sought to pin my wavering beliefs. Here was a self-description of a reluctant follower of a God who seemed determined to place demands on those who had hoped to avoid his notice and continue their lives uninterrupted by the attentions of his interest. Indeed, in his book, Jeremiah comes across as a man of deep sensitivity and loyalty who, despite himself, is called to deliver a prophetic message that is neither welcome nor heeded, and for whom the cost of being true to himself is bitter suffering. Such loyalty, and the price of it, which included being placed in the stocks, being incarcerated in a muddy well, and solitary imprisonment, is drawn out in response to the compelling purpose of the shape of God's own fidelity.

Most of Jeremiah's book appears to be written by his faithful scribe Baruch, though there may be other scribes and other additions. The chronology is all at sixes and sevens as the author makes clear at the beginning of the book. The words cover several reigns. The encounter with God, which makes the call a reality, does not appear to be set in a particular context, though it appears to be a description of a real event early in Jeremiah's life.

Jeremiah lived through a period of enormous political upheaval. He is a citizen of Judah, the Southern Kingdom. He appears to come from a priestly family who own land in the town of Anathoth, a few miles to the north east of Jerusalem. His period of prophecy runs from the years 627 to 587 BC, when Jerusalem was sacked and the majority of the people, especially the educated and influential members of the community, were taken into slavery by Nebuchadnezzar, the warrior ruler of the Babylonian empire. In the course of the period, Jeremiah knew the reign of the young King Josiah, who made a vigorous attempt to revitalise and reform the religious life of the community. In 621

a new scroll of the Law was discovered hidden in the wall of
the temple, and Josiah, aided by the high priest, Hilkiah,
made determined efforts to resuscitate the religious values
and faithfulness of the Jewish tradition. His reign was backed
by the political ferment of the day, in which the separated
Southern Kingdom of Judah found itself vulnerable both
politically and geographically. The Assyrian empire, which
had subjugated the Northern Kingdom of Israel, was in
decline, and being rivalled for hegemony by the rising star of
the Babylonian empire, and by the power of Egypt. Josiah fell
at the battle of Megiddo holding the plain against Egyptian
forces in 609; and in 605, the Babylonians defeated the
Egyptians at the battle of Carchemish. Josiah was succeeded
by the tyrannical and ruthless Jehoiakim, whose unwise
alliances and irresponsible posturing led to the first invasion
of Jerusalem in 597. Nebuchadnezzar then appointed
Zedekiah as regent. He appears to have been a weak, if not
unkindly ruler, but his defiance of Babylonian authority was
to lead to the siege of Jerusalem, the sacking of the city, the
exile of the Jewish people, and his own personal captivity
and blinding in 587.

Such is the background of Jeremiah's call to prophecy. His
own political acumen could tell him of the nature of the vulnerability of the Judean state and the folly of the policies of
its rulers, aided and advised by a series of worldly and
myopic false prophets. Given both the history and the experience of religious faithlessness, and involvement with
Canaanite fertility cults, and the social injustice of the community, Jeremiah, like others of the prophets, is clear that it
is the apostasy and waywardness of the people that will bring
its own retribution and divine punishment. He sees God as
retributive and yet merciful. In his famous parable of the potter in chapter 18, he compares God to a master potter able
to make, break, or remake his people as a potter works with
his clay. In chapters 30–33, Jeremiah's vision of recovery and
renewal, of the new action of God in a future hope, is powerful and optimistic, full of a sense of hope among conditions
of despair. Again and again, he is called to warn, to chide, to

advise, to admonish. For his efforts, he receives constant abuse, punishment and vilification. There is something deeply heroic about this sensitive and compassionate man called, despite himself, to a prophetic role, in which the dictates of religious fidelity and political awareness mean that he courts disaster. He is the victim of his own vision. He is demonised for the truth he proclaims. He pays the price of his own vocation.

The story of Jeremiah's call must have come out of the depths of his own experience. What does it tell us about the contour of God?

First of all, there are many echoes of previous encounters. Jeremiah appears to hear that same sense of personal selection heard by Moses who, like him, was known. Jeremiah hears that he has been 'known'[2] from the moment of conception. He is told that his relationship with God began in the pre-consciousness days of the security of his mother's womb. To be known is to be consecrated. To be consecrated is to be sent. Like Moses, Jeremiah is full of trepidation and lack of confidence at the challenge of his selection and appointment. 'Ah Lord God! Behold I do not know how to speak, for I am only a youth'.[3] Such protestations are overruled with the promise of the enabling grace of God and, like Joshua, he is promised protection, skill and courage. Like Isaiah of Jerusalem, Jeremiah, faced by his own sense of inadequacy and reluctance, finds himself reconstituted by some form of symbolic cleansing of his mouth: 'Behold, I have put my words in your mouth: See, I have set you this day over nations and kingdoms'.[4]

Jeremiah's record of his encounter is offered, by inference, in the light of subsequent events and vicissitudes. His authenticity as a prophet is validated by the certainty of his vocation. Indeed the story of the book is the story of a reluctant and badly used prophet, who pays a high price for the conviction that this sense of righteousness and justice and personal conviction must be proclaimed whatever the personal cost. The contour presented to us by the text of Jeremiah's call is of a vocational God; a God who singles out those whom he requires for his kingdom, and who places a particular demand on that requirement.

Vocation is a most complicated part of religious experience. The testimony of the stories of encounters with God all present a sense of personal call and identity. Jesus specifically called particular apostles and particular disciples. The Christian centuries are a testimony to the vocation of countless Christian men and women who have believed themselves called to particular ministries, and to creative and reforming tasks. Equally, it can be possible to see how a sense of personal vocation is open to misjudgment, delusion and self-deception. There are many ways in which it is possible to fantasise about ideals or motivation. Self-interest can present itself in the disguise of a high calling. Furthermore, a sense of vocation can change. It is possible, presumably, for God's own initiatory designs to change with the on-goingness of human experience and development.

One example of vocational misjudgment would appear to be the vision of Father Ignatius, (the Revd Joseph Leycaster Lyne) who lived from 1837–1908. This eccentric missionary deacon had difficulty finding a bishop prepared to ordain him priest, until 1898. Then hands were laid upon him by the bizarre figure of 'Mar Timotheus', a French Roman Catholic turned Protestant, who became a bishop in Colombo, Ceylon, on the strength of a forged Papal Bull. Father Ignatius conceived that his vocation was to revive the Benedictine order in the Anglican Church. He persuaded a number of Victorian gentrified ladies, especially in parishes in the West Country, to back his scheme financially. Eventually his extensive monastery in the Black Mountains on the Welsh border housed three brethren. The uncompleted ruins of the Abbey church above the tiny hamlet at Capel-y-ffin, where Ignatius lies buried, stand as a bleak testimony to a vocation lost in the eccentricities of personal, rather than divine, vision.

Testing vocation is a skilled and delicate task where the need for the grace of the Holy Spirit is such an essential prerequisite. Wise and experienced help from those steeped in their own spiritual journey is crucial. Individualism can be a serious blind, and it is only by persistent prayer that vocational enlightenment can be sought.

In the words of the ordinal in the Church of England, a candidate is asked by the ordaining bishop: 'Do you believe, so far as you known your own heart, that God has called you to the office and work ...?[5] Somewhat disappointingly, in the order of confirmation which surely ought to be seen as a form of commissioning of lay vocation, no direct question of this kind is put. The questions are about repentance and about faith. Perhaps the methods of preparing people for confirmation are too deeply associated with teaching and recruitment and insufficiently alive to the nature of a vocational God.

It is in the nature of God to call and to appoint. Jeremiah was, of course, called into a task of daunting difficulty. Some Christian people will know something of the demands of that kind of vocation. For many others, a religious allegiance may be more to do with association with a cultural or social club, with finding a way of self-authentication in a difficult world where other groups have been rejecting or marginalising. Of course, a Christian community, if it is to be true to its corporate Christian vision, must seek to be a community of welcome, a community of openness and friendship, unashamedly 'a home for lost dogs', a hospital for emotional and psychological disorder; but there will be dangers if that community of open acceptance loses sight of the contour of the vocational God. We are not called just to be befrienders, or visitors, or community organisers, or the local welfare group or curators of buildings. We are called into a fellowship of prayer and worship, into a relationship with a God who says: 'Before I formed you in the womb I knew you, and before you were born I consecrated you'.[6]

A new incumbent was appointed to a parish where there lived an ex-churchwarden who had held his office for well over twenty years. His faithfulness to his duties had been exemplary and he had worshipped twice a Sunday without fail, and given hours of his time to maintaining the fabric of the church. He had resigned as churchwarden before the new appointment and there was no story of disaffection or ill-will. Indeed his financial support of the church was maintained. Since the time of his resignation, he chose to worship on only very rare occasions in the parish church which he had cared for so faithfully for so long, while remaining welcoming and interested to those who called on him. How had vocation to God been perceived over those years of church-wardenly faithfulness?

It is part of the contour of God to call us into a life of personal encounter which will be demanding, exhilarating, daunting and at times threatening. The story of Jeremiah is the story of vocation at continued cost. Just as the church-warden returned to his bees having fulfilled his duties so faithfully, so might this faithful, vulnerable man have longed to base his life round the family estates of Anathoth. There, Jeremiah could have developed a pastoral and family existence, allowing the tides of war and the political turmoils of the day to swirl round him, excusing himself on the reasonable ground that his particular view of theological and political events would be neither listened to nor of influence. Instead Jeremiah commits his life to proclaiming a prophetic message, which is unpopular and, as a result, invokes intimidation.

It is the mark of Jeremiah's vocation that he is convinced of God's faithfulness and of the quality of his relationship with him, even in the midst of all kinds of calamities and dangers. In chapters 30–33, he proclaims a conviction that in the midst of all the very considerable military and political dangers, there will be a future, when the activity of God's love will be shown in redemption and restoration. He believes convincedly that, although there might be a terrible shattering of the imperfect clay pot of Israelite infidelity, that very shattering will be the resource for re-creation and renewal, under a new covenant.

In chapter 32 there is an astonishing example of personal faith and conviction under the grace of a vocational God. Jeremiah would have identified with the words of St Paul to the Romans: 'And those whom he called, he also justified; and those whom he justified, he also glorified'.[7] It is a time of incredible hardship. The Chaldean army has virtually surrounded the city of Jerusalem. There is virtually no food in the city. Jeremiah is himself in prison, for fear that his warnings will demoralise a cowed population further. Word reaches him that, as next of kin, he has the right to buy his cousin's field in the family city of Anathoth. This he does, putting the deeds into safe keeping, in an earthenware vessel. He declares before the witnesses of the purchase: 'For thus says the Lord of hosts, the God of Israel: Houses and fields and vineyards shall again be bought in this land'.[8] The purchase of the field is an outward and visible sign of faith in the future and of personal conviction in his vocation.

In 1940, when I was a few weeks old, my father and his brother were both serving in the British Expeditionary Force, becoming increasingly isolated and surrounded as the force retreated towards the town of Dunkirk. Little news was available about the safety of individual members of the retreating army. In the context of the early summer of that year, the dangers of invasion and subjugation under a Nazi tyranny must have seemed very great. At such a time, my mother went out to purchase a rocking horse for her new baby which became a well-loved and well-used family friend. I have always seen it as an example of faithfulness in the future and of the conviction that in all things God will be God.

It is one of the convictions of Julian of Norwich that God is 'able to make everything well' and that 'all manner of things shall be well'.[9] Her own historical context in 14th century England, surrounded by the black death, the privations of the concluding hundred years war, the corruption of the medieval Church, and a succession of bad harvests, did not make for great optimism. Unequivocally, Julian is hopeful for the future. In the future is God. He who calls will be faithful. All that shall befall, including sin, has a necessary purpose. What may seem incomprehensible, alarming, unstable now, will in the future reveal a purpose and a fruition.

Christian hope is not a form of blind and bland optimism which foolishly looks for unrealistic solutions in the midst of a complex and dangerous world. Christian hope has at its root a perception about the contour of God which is creatively vocational. For reasons which we shall never know nor understand, it is within the capacity of God to place his hand upon us, as Jeremiah reveals it, into the very heart of our foetal state. Having placed his hand upon us, as St Augustine puts it, our hearts will be restless until they rest in him.[10]

In the account in Acts Chapter 9 of the conversion of St Paul, a disciple named Ananias, who lives at Damascus, is told to go to the newly-converted Paul in his blind state, and authenticate his new ministry. When Ananias demurs, understandably uncertain of such a change in Pauline behaviour, he hears the words: 'Go, for he is a chosen instrument of mine to carry my name before the Gentiles and kings and the sons of Israel'.[11]

It is part of the contour of God to be a 'chooser of his instruments'. The story of Jeremiah is the story of being chosen. One of the tasks of Christian discipleship is the task of keeping fresh and alert the vocation we might believe we have received. An ingredient in that freshness and alertness is to be faithful about the future even when that future may look bemusedly uncertain and fraught with challenge and change.

In Kahlil Gibran's book *The Prophet*, the conclusion speaks of 'the Master's' departure. Here the holy, central figure of the book who has spoken on so many matters of human experience takes leave of his people:

> 'After saying these things he looked about him, and he saw the pilot of his ship standing by the helm and gazing now at the full sails, and now at the distance. And he said:
> "Patient, over patient, is the captain of my ship. The wind blows and restless are the sails; even the rudder begs direction; yet quietly my captain awaits my silence.

And these my mariners, who have heard the choir of the
greater sea, they too have heard me patiently".
Now they shall wait no longer. I am ready.' [12]

Chapter 12

An Initiatory God:

Ezekiel's Vision of the
High Pastures of Israel

(Ezekiel 34. 11–16)

IT WAS when visiting the remarkable mosaic from an early
Islamic art form, at Hisham's Palace near Jericho, that the
words heard by Ezekiel truly struck me. Looking up at the
surrounding hills in late spring, the green patches of pasture
dazzled in the sunshine, and the heights of Israel became dappled by the shadows of clouds. There was a cragginess and a
robustness, there was an invitation in those crags. Something
about the way the green of the grass and the greyness of the
rock combined in the sunlight, and all up high, made for a
sense of being surrounded by the powerfulness of the land,
and gave out a glimpse of the ancient visions of the prophets
and psalmists.

Ezekiel's oracle about the initiative of God in Chapter 34
was declared in the year 587 BC. He tells us in the previous
chapter that he had been in exile for twelve years and that
news of the fall of Jerusalem, after a long siege, had been
brought. Ezekiel was of the priestly caste, probably of the
house of Zadok, the high priest of the Solomonic era.
Aristocratic, cultured, educated, he had been one of the first
of the exiled Jews to be transported to Babylon following the
first sacking of the city in 598, which had included the capture of King Jehoiakim.

In exile, and living in a house of his own, amongst other
transported Jews, by the River Chebar, Ezekiel experienced a
series of visions. Many of these seem extraordinary and
weird. He seems either to have returned to Jerusalem at some
stage, or to have been kept very well informed of events in
the city. At one point in his book, he seems to have been
transported back to Jerusalem in spirit[1] and there, he is confronted by the cultic and political disorder practised under

the regency of Zedekiah. He sees himself as a watchman appointed by God to call the people to a new vision of holiness and religious purity.

The period of the exile became an enormously strong influence in the forging of a Jewish religious identity that would flourish again when, in due course, the exiles would return. Ezekiel calls for an individual response and a sense of personal commitment to a new hope and a new future, because God's power would be vindicated in his action. It is the same prophetic message as appears in Jeremiah and second Isaiah, though the reasons for God's will to action vary in their interpretation.

Much of Ezekiel's prophecies tell of a direct encounter with God, who appears to speak to him direct and who often addresses him as 'Son of Man', perhaps a way of emphasising his mortality in contrast to the holiness of God. His knowledge of God and his communication from God appear to be both extensive and wide- ranging.The story of his original call in chapter 1 is full of fanciful imagery but there is an implicit authenticity in the acceptance that the word of the Lord had come to him.[2]

In chapter 34, the word of the Lord comes to Ezekiel again, as on other occasions. In the first 10 verses of the chapter, he is at pains to castigate the false shepherds and religious leaders of the day for their corruption and venality. In the last section there is given a Messianic vision of both a restoration at the hands of a 'new Shepherd' and a vision of the new order to be implemented as a result of God's action, comparable to the visions of the Isaiahs and Jeremiah. In the middle, verses 11–16, there is vouchsafed a contour of God which is precious and important. It is the image of a God who initiates his own action in order to feed and pasture his sheep.

The image of sheep and shepherd is a repetitive one in both the Old Testament and the New Testament. Jesus used the image on a number of occasions and his presentation of himself as the Good Shepherd in John 10 is a key presentation in the 'I am' sayings in the Gospel.[3]

This image still carries a sense of something important about God and how we see him. In the British Isles, sheep have for long played a very important part in the husbandry and economy of our islands. There are many parts of the country where sheep alone are productive even in times of agricultural recession. Their capacity to gain food from areas of poor grass and moorland make them an inevitable part of large tracts of wild land, while they graze efficiently, too, in large parts of richer pastureland.

There remains something remarkably disconnected to many people's modern everyday life in the presence of flocks of sheep. In part this may be through association with places of wildness and detachment. The sound of sheep, the presence of lambs, the sight of their existence, all have a way of contributing to a sense of something different to ourselves. Perhaps in part it is biblical images which are in the background, in our response to sheep. Sheep farmers may well have a very different view, but for many there is an intangible 'something' about the presence of flocks of grazing sheep.

Ezekiel presents his perception of the people as like sheep, as Jesus would so do in years to come and in the same way as, for him, the people are as sheep without a shepherd, harassed and helpless.[4]

So much of our human experience is one of harassment and helplessness. We feel pressured by many demands and expectations. For some, working life can become a succession of too many requirements to be fulfilled. We can feel harassed by shortage of money, incomplete relationships, the repetition of our mistakes, the demands which others put upon us. We can feel victimised by our inability to reorder our lives to avoid the harassment which is often partly of our own making and partly heaped upon us.

Sheep grazing peacefully on the moorland may well have a mystical quality. Sheep being herded in all their sense of aimlessness and obtuseness come nearer to our appreciation of how our lives can become. Our directions hard to find; committed to following others whose leadership capacities we doubt; pushed hither and thither by forces we cannot easily control; trapped into routes that appear aimless and reduced, we can feel like harassed sheep. Into the harassment comes the helplessness. However we try to turn our situation, each new perspective becomes as blind as the next. We become victims of our own situation, saddled with the ingredients of our own making and often contributory to our own treadmill. It becomes impossible to find a way out of, or through, the disorder of our lives. We have the wish to make changes but doubt the capacity or the will. Some of this feeling of harassment and helplessness can project on to God a conception that we are pawns in a wider divine chess game, expendable and without profit. God can be perceived as like a gigantic cat playing inconsequentially with his mice.

Ezekiel, like others of the prophets, is convinced that the people have brought their own misfortunes upon themselves. He also believes that God will yet rescue and redeem his chosen people, in part, in Ezekiel's view, to demonstrate something of his power and glory to a world hooked on to false gods.

It is, despite our suspicion of Ezekiel's reasoning, an axiom of religious faith that God does act and will act. It is hard in the light of the complexity of scientific evidence to hold any of the more traditional views of an interventionist and availably controlling contour to God. New insights in physics and biology seem to be pointing to a much more complex and unplanned order to the material world. It is now recognised that the world is so complicatedly inter-related as to offer extraordinary manifestations of unbelievably wide chance, leading to processes and life-forms almost, but not quite, statistically impossible. It is, none the less, a clear part of Christian experience that God does seem to make himself available to the infinite range of human needs and sorrows and that availability is not simply a wishful thought in a coincidence-experiencing vision. Thousands would testify to the unexplained reality of response and answer in the midst of all our stresses and strains, our hopes and fears, our excitements and disappointments.

When Ezekiel heard God saying that he himself would

search for his sheep and seek them out, he was expressing a true religious experience. It is a real part of the contour of God to seek us and to find us. He is discoverable in the journey of life and it is a strange ingredient to our experience that God seems to engineer the means to confront us and to use us. We may seek for him only in our lostness and sense of forlornness, but his search for us is persistent and indefatigable.

In *Four Quartets*, in the section on Little Gidding, T S Eliot writes:

> 'What we call the beginning is often the end
> And to make an end is to make a beginning.
> The end is where we start from.
>
> ...
>
> With the drawing of this Love and the voice of this
>   Calling
> We shall not cease from our exploration
> And the end of all our exploring
> Will be to arrive where we started
> And know the place for the first time'.[5]

I remember once on a fine May morning worshipping in the ancient Saxon church at Corhampton in Hampshire, which has outside the door a gnarled and extensive yew tree, reputedly original to the church and believed to have existed in the churchyard before William the Conqueror landed in 1066. There is always something enormously stable and encouraging about a living thing which is very old. The old church itself contains medieval wall paintings, a Norman door and evidence of Saxon walls. It was for long the parish church of the village of Lomer, which became a plague village, and can be seen only in the mounds of the foundations underneath farmland. On the roof is usually perched a colony of pigeons who accompany the divine office with their own background of cooing and fluttering. Their continuous existence provides a symbolic contribution to the experience of the persistent presence of the Holy Spirit, active and alive throughout all time.

On this particular morning, walking home with other worshippers, we crossed the River Meon and were met by a mother duck leading a concourse of some twenty ducklings. She rushed towards us, flapping her wings in delight, quacking with joy, and the ducklings excitedly followed, cheeping and pressing in a mass of yellow enthusiasm. The rush towards people was infectious and overwhelming. 'Here we are', the ducks seemed to say, 'We are here and we love you and we welcome you and we share with you'.

Now of course there is nothing sacrosanct in itself about the world of nature, and not long after the experience, I saw another duck trying determinedly, but unsuccessfully, to drown ducklings in the river. In the sense that there is a manifestation of God in the natural world, as we sometimes perceive it, and as it can reflect the glory and the joy of God, there seemed to be something about the encounter with the mother duck and her brood, which seemed also to say something about the way God seeks us out. 'Look! Here I am! Have you noticed me?' The truth is, of course, that so often we have not noticed him. We have become so absorbed in our own particular personal or corporate disorder that we have failed to see.

Ezekiel, as he reflects on an encounter with God in the middle of chapter 34, speaks of a God who will take the initiative to search out his sheep wherever they may have been scattered. It is more than probable that Jesus reflected on this passage, which would have been well known in his synagogue experience, when he told the parable of the lost sheep out of the hundred in the flock.

The search is to involve a gathering. Again, it is possible that this passage was the root of Jesus' cry of anguish on the Mount of Olives, on the first Palm Sunday,[6] when he wept over the city, and his declaration earlier that he so longed to gather the people as a hen gathers her brood under her wings. [7]

Julian of Norwich, at a number of points in her Revelations, but particularly in Revelations 59 and 61, speaks of Christ as 'our Mother'. Here she develops the concept of the second person of the Trinity as both the source of wisdom, from the wisdom literature, and as a source of overshadowing and enfolding, as revealed in the world of matter; 'Thus Jesus is our true Mother in nature, from our first creation, and He is our true Mother in grace, by His taking our created human nature' (Revelation 59).[8] She develops further the idea that God is both father and mother. 'As truly as God is our Father, so truly God is our Mother' (Revelation 59).[9]

The shepherding quality of God's contour and shape in the encounter in Ezekiel 34 has a parenting quality that is without gender and should be without consequent prejudice. The contour presented is of the nature of God which will itself respond in tenderness and love, in initiative and 'parental' concern for all who are the subject of his adoration and concern. There is to be a bringing out and a gathering. There is to be a searching and a rescuing.

Irina Ratushinskaya tells in her book *Grey is the colour of hope* of her experience as a Christian political prisoner in communist Russia. It is a testimony of struggle and fortitude, shared with other prisoners, some criminal and some political, in the face of a de-humanising system. She speaks of the 'third side involved in the conflict: all those people who were campaigning for our freedom: in Russia, Ukraine, Lithuania, Britain, Sweden, the USA ... Oh, that I could list them all, and name everybody by name! ... people ... who demonstrated outside Soviet embassies, gathered signatures under petitions, prayed for us. It was this third side which decided the ultimate outcome of the war, forcing open the gate of the camp'.[10]

Towards the conclusion of the account, at the culmination of a succession of privations, in solitary confinement, and near the end of her resources, she speaks of 'a strange warmth stands over what is left of my body and I rock to the crooning of a lullaby ... I did not know, then, that on that very day a service of intercession was being held for me in a far-off English city'.[11] There have been other testimonies to the ability to recognise and receive the power of prayer and concern from heroic sufferers undergoing desperate miseries at the hands of tyrannical prison systems. Again, the testimony seems to be of a strange and unexpected warmth flowing in from beyond.

Once I was taken into hospital after an injury at home, and, with little time to collect immediate needs, I grabbed the nearest book to hand, which turned out to be Kahlil Gibran's *Jesus, Son of Man*. There is a moving passage in that account of Jesus' earthly ministry where the author puts into the mouth of Christ at the Last Supper, words presented as being remembered by James, the brother of the Lord: 'Let not your heart be troubled. I only leave you to prepare a place for you in my Father's house. But if you shall be in need of me, I will come back to you. Where you call me, there I shall hear you, and wherever your spirit shall seek me, there I will be'.[12] In the loneliness of a hospital ward bed, the words offered a powerful reassurance.

It is the quality of Christian experience to find that God does search us out and he does find us. The initiative is his. The searching is not in itself to be enough. The finding is to lead to seeking, and the finding will involve the binding up and the healing of all who are vulnerable or lost. In the account of the feeding of the five thousand in St Mark and St Luke, Jesus is reported to have said to the disciples, when the problem of the hungry multitude and the late hour was first raised: 'You give them something to eat'.[13]

So, within the contours of God, is born the vision of the Church for which, within the grace of the power of God, there is need to include the co-operation of humankind to enable the feeding and the binding. One of the most moving expressions of mutual feeding and support is to be found in the 4th century mosaic at Tabgha, the alleged site of the miracle of the feeding of the five thousand. Here, all the animals and birds of the region are depicted. On one of the panels of the mosaic, a heron is feeding, with its beak, a rock badger. The two great prayers of St Teresa of Avila encapsulate this double energy: 'Christ has no hands on earth but your hands

now', and 'He who has God, finds he lacks nothing: God
alone suffices'.[14]

The initiative and energy is God's. He is the feeder and
provider. Those who commit themselves to his sustaining
grace find themselves resourced and enabled in a way that is
valid only on the yardstick of experience. Many may feel
uneasy that much of the Old Testament teaching seems to
imply blessing in proportional abundance to the measure of
gifting, as if there could be a quid pro quo in the munificence
of God's bounty. The reality nearer the mark lies in the teaching of Jesus that the measure you give will be the measure
you receive, and still more will be given to you.[15]

Ezekiel, the exile in the land of Babylon, a refugee from his
homeland and a prisoner of a foreign régime, dreams of the
high pastures of Israel. There is an echo of Robert
Browning's poem:

> 'O to be in England
> Now that April's there,
> And whoever wakes in England
> Sees, some morning, unaware,
> That the lowest boughs and the brushwood sheaf,
> Round the elm-tree bole are in tiny leaf,
> While the chaffinch sings on the orchard bough
> in England – now!'[16]

for Ezekiel it is: 'And I will feed them on the mountains of
Israel, by the fountains, and in all the inhabited places of the
country. I will feed them with good pasture, and upon the
mountain heights of Israel shall be their pasture; there they
shall lie down in good grazing land, and on fat pasture they
shall feed on the mountains of Israel.'[17] Surrounded by the
deserts and waterways of the Babylonian heartland, perhaps
Ezekiel fantasised upon the range of hills that surround the
Jericho area, in their time of spring.

Ezekiel described himself as a watchman (Ezekiel 3.17, &
33.6). He or she who would perceive something of the initiatory nature of God must follow the calling of the watchman. It is significant that, in the ordinal of the Church of

England prayer book, in the words of the Bishop's Charge, the candidates are told to be 'messengers, watchmen, stewards of the Lord'.[18]

In the medieval and the ancient city, the watchman fulfilled a crucial role for the wellbeing of the citizens. His was the task of preserving the safety of the community. He patrolled the walls, scanning the horizons beyond, sensitive to any evidence of danger and alert to the weather, to change, to news, to external initiative.

The task of any Christian minister, ordained or lay, is to be a watchperson, on the outlook for signs of the presence of God. It is very easy to be sleepy in the watches of the night. It is very easy to miss the signals, the signs, and the spoor of the presence of God. His initiatives often go unnoticed. The watchman must be alert while others sleep. The watchman must interpret the evidence of the presence of what is new, challenging, and decisive; for the God of Ezekiel is not a passive, unconcerned, disengaged God, but the shepherd of his sheep who declares, 'Behold, I, I myself will search for my sheep, and will seek them out. As a shepherd seeks out his flock when some of his sheep have been scattered abroad, so will I seek out my sheep; and I will rescue them from all places where they have been scattered on a day of clouds and thick darkness.' [19]

Chapter 13

The Pro-Active God:
The Faithfulness of Second-Isaiah
(Isaiah 49. 1–6)

THERE IS such a wealth of thought and vision in the writings of Second-Isaiah (Isaiah 40–55), and much of his writings speak of so close a relationship with God that the selection of one passage to portray an encounter, to describe a contour for God, is bound to be arbitrary. The early part of chapter 49 is a watershed in Isaiah's thought. He describes his call, somewhat in the same terms as Jeremiah, and the passage appears to be one of the so-called 'Servant Songs'. The poetry in these passages is resonant with a sense of the activity of God at work in his world, using his servant for his own redemptive purposes. It is never clear whether the 'Suffering Servant' is an unknown individual, Isaiah himself, the Israelite community, or another community, perhaps one envisaged by the author. The expressed conviction is centred more on what God can and will do, than exactly through whom he will do it, though there is a real sense of belief that power will be expressed through weakness, sorrow and suffering. The 'Servant' will become an instrument of glory and hope, through the power of God at work in his world. Vicarious suffering will be redemptive. It seems certain that Jesus identified closely with the prophecy of Second Isaiah. Christian thought has been greatly influenced by Isaiah's theology.

The context of his writing is the mid-6th century, when the Jewish people are in exile in Babylon, following the fall of Jerusalem in 587 BC. It would seem that the exiles lived out some kind of life of corporate identity under Babylonian rule, and it is possible that life was reasonably secure and even comfortable. Jewish craftsmen would have brought their skills. The empire of Nebuchadnezzar was comparatively benevolent. There are no tales of harsh slavery such as in the great oppression in Egypt. None the less, this second exile is seen as a profound debacle for Jewish identity. The collapse

first of the Northern Kingdom and then of Judah under-
mined any concept of nationhood. Memories of Jerusalem
and the cultic worship of old Israel would have been preserved, and there were longing hopes for restoration and
return.

Fulfilment of such hopefulness became a real possibility
with the rise of the Persian empire under Cyrus. The Babylonian or Median empire was fragmenting from within, especially under the weak and unpopular rule of Nabodinus,
though in the year 561, under Nebuchadnezzar's successor,
Amel-Marduk, Jehoiachin, the legitimate heir to the Davidic
throne, had been released from prison. After a series of vic-
torious campaigns which enlarged the Persian empire well
into Asia Minor, Cyrus fought the Babylonians at the battle
of Opis in 539 BC and the shadow of Nebuchadnezzar was
expunged for ever. Cyrus appears to have been an unusually
benevolent despot, especially in the context of his age, and it
was under his authority that the Jewish exiles began their
return home.

Second-Isaiah perceived the political wind of change as
constructive and hopeful and saw Cyrus as an instrument of
God's providence and activity. His writings appear to fall
into two halves, and Isaiah 49 begins a second stage in the
evolution of his thought.

In Isaiah 40–48, the author lays out his vision of hope and
promise. Seeing God as deeply involved and active in the creative processes of history, he forecasts new things for the people. God will act. He will reveal his glory. His power will be
manifest. In poetic language of very great beauty, he equates
the activity of God with the revelation of God in the natural
world. So, deserts will spring into pools of water. Highways
will be levelled across mountains. Green shoots will appear
in wastelands. A holistic vision of change and beauty and
resource and goodness will break out into the darkness and
despair of exiles in a strange land.

It is possible that Second-Isaiah would have declared
something of his vision of hope as an individual preacher and
sage, holding forth in the market places and centres of gath-

ering of the Jewish communities. Probably his message was conveyed by disciples in synagogues and in households. His poetry is resonant with the context of harsh hills, desert places and stony ground, and with the memory of a lush past and of remembered beauty and natural harmony. Some of this thinking must have been coloured by the perception of the corporate memory of the past and the pressure of an exiled existence. At the heart of Second-Isaiah's thought lies a deep conviction that God is active, concerned, powerful and will change things for the better.

By the second half of the book, beginning with chapter 49, a sense of disillusionment seems to have crept into his thinking. It seems that exiles had begun to return to Jerusalem. Divisions were apparently already arising between the theology of Second-Isaiah, whose perception was one of inclusion and of a sense of Jewish vocation to be a missionary faith, and of others, possibly disciples of the school of Ezekiel, who were working for a more narrow and exclusive vision of the Jewish religious message. In all his writings, Second-Isaiah, if it is indeed he who wrote all of Isaiah 40–55, proclaims a conviction about the dynamic activity of God. This activity is interventionist, pro-active, resourcing history and politics, and revealed through the on-going creativity expressed in both the natural world and human affairs.

Second-Isaiah must have been a man deeply rooted in a faith both stable and dynamic. His personal encounters with God appear to have had a spiritual reality, which certainly shines through his writings. For Second-Isaiah, God was a real and living force and a relationship with him would lead to change and transformation. In years to come when the Messianic sects, typified by the Essene Community at Qumran, began to proclaim the imminent fulfilment of Isaiah's prophecies, and transcribed his writings, the copyist would never write the name of God without a ritual cleansing of his hand. This powerful, this active, this holy was the God of Second-Isaiah! What kind of contour of God does Isaiah 49. 1–6 teach?

First of all, along with so many encounters with God in the

Old Testament, Isaiah is called into a relationship with God from the moment of conception, and by name. Here is a God who relates individually and personally, who calls, who enables, and who has a purpose for his servants. Second-Isaiah has no doubt about his personal vocation. God singles out and connects. Indeed, he is the giver of gifts and talents and he will use them, making mouths like sharp swords, and human-beings like polished arrows. If there is an enabling quality about the vitality of call, there is also a protective quality. God shadows and conceals.

There is much in Old Testament thought about over-shadowing, enclosing and incorporating. It is an important dimension to a perception of the nature of God. In his imminence, God is closer than hands and feet. He is about us. He surrounds us. He is part of us. The image of being like a polished arrow in a quiver has its own somewhat whimsical language to teach us about selection, about potential usefulness and about protection. God has a purpose for us. In his strength, we can become polished and effective. We are resourced by his protection.

'And He said to me: You are my servant Israel in whom I will be glorified'.[1] Second-Isaiah seems to mingle personal vocation with corporate vocation to an extent which it is difficult to decipher. Perhaps there is no need! The call of God will, by its very nature, be personal in terms of its sense of being one-to-one; and corporate in the sense of being elastic as to how we are to fulfil that vocation. John Donne's famous sermon in which he proclaimed that 'no man is an island'[2] is a constant reproach to any vision of God that sees the spiritual life as isolated from a relationship with others, and divorced from a context within the life of whatever section of the world community the believer may be living within. Part of Isaiah's thinking encouraged him to re-emphasise the vocation of the whole people to be a light to lighten the gentiles.

Christmas gives Christians in Northern Europe a wonderful opportunity to symbolise the vision of Second-Isaiah. Many churches hold candlelight services and/or Christingle

services. There is a very simple truth in the symbolism of the
passing of candlelight. One candle burning alone in the darkness of a church, large or small, has a heroic fragility about
it. It is a brave and certainly powerful expression of determined brightness in the darkness of the world.

Tiny light never being overcome by darkness is expressed
powerfully in the ceremony of the Easter Fire on Holy
Saturday when the 'Light of Christ' is born into the dark
church. As at Christmas, it is the exchange of light which can
so transform: candlelight passed from person to person,
everyone lighting from each other, the magnification of one
tiny light into hundreds of lights. This is a symbolic way of
expressing the fusion of the individual and the corporate in
the life of faith.

Second-Isaiah speaks of a God who calls individuals into
community so that a shared enterprise may change and transform. It is one of the tragedies of faith communities that the
combination of individualism and the collective so often
leads to fragmentation. In Second-Isaiah's thought, the two
aspirations go hand in hand. The history of organised religion will tell of schisms and disputes, of faction and at times
civil war. Unscrupulous political leaders have often found
ready ways of harnessing religious differences to further
national and tribal antagonisms. In the thinking of Second-
Isaiah, the servant and the people share a common vocation
to be a light to the nations.

The full shape of the contours of God are bound to be too
complex and unfathomable for individual perception to
grasp. For Second-Isaiah, there has to be a fusion of individualism and corporateness for true spiritual vocation to be
found. This paradoxical insight has a message for the modern Church showing, as it does, signs of polarised sectional-
ism.

So often, Christian communities seem to develop their own
individualistic life which forms the pattern of some kind of
ritualistic club. Here the rules of the membership develop a
persona of their own. 'Here at St so and so's we do things in
this way ... We call ourselves a continuing Church or a tra-

ditional Church, or a progressive Church. We are a Catholic Church or an Evangelical Church or a renewed Church. We believe in this or we believe in that. We practise a particular form of religious observance. We can even advertise our particular brand.'

In such a club, the minister becomes a chairperson of importance but the real power lies in the hands of an elite membership, often people with powerful personalities and/or long purses. 'Belonging' will be about learning the rules and observances of the club. Asking questions or making suggestions will not be seen as a welcome contribution. Openness and inclusiveness will be seen as dangerous to 'the tradition', and the shape of the community will seem, therefore, inaccessible to those outside it. Membership will seem difficult to achieve and will appear to depend on passing various tests and learning new customs, behaviour patterns and language.

Perhaps it was some of these forces at work among the returning exiles to Jerusalem which made Second-Isaiah despair and declare: 'I have laboured in vain, I have spent my strength for nothing and vanity'.[3] That sense of personal inadequacy and failure, of depression and loss of self-worth, which seems to be a repeated feature in direct encounters with God, emerges, albeit paralleled with an affirmation of God's continued 'recompense'.

The shape of God which Second-Isaiah perceives, however, is pro-active and determined. It wastes no time on a personal sense of inadequacy. It reconstitutes. It reaffirms. It calls. It enables. It has a purpose. It honours. It gives the individual as a light to the nations that 'my salvation may reach to the end of the earth'.[4] It uses the individual to facilitate the corporate: 'So I rose to honour in the Lord's sight and my God became my glory'.[5]

The thinking of Second-Isaiah raises the whole question as to whether God actively intervenes in his world to 'fulfil his purpose'. Second-Isaiah clearly believed that God not only did but would. Modern Christianity seems to divide itself increasingly between the more fundamentalist or semi-fundamentalist views of tradition and scripture, where the miraculous is the norm; and the 'open Christian' view which tends to discount the paranormal and 'miraculous' view of God's activity and to see the activity of God as expressed in all acts of faithful endeavour and in the normality of every-day experience, where divine evidence is to be found not in the extraordinary but in the ordinary. In both, the power and reality of resurrection are affirmed, but where one view looks for 'signs and wonders', the other view is unable to counte-nance any idea of God 'intervening' into the natural laws and processes of the world.

The contour of God which Second-Isaiah presents to his readers is one of a pro-active God if not an interventionist God. For him, God is a real changer of the world. God will act. God will change. God will restore. God will redeem.

It must be possible for the person of faith whatever their perspective to apprehend a contour of God which is indeed pro-active. On the one hand this must be delivered from the obscurantist concept of a puppet-master type of God, wield-ing his magic this way and that, who is constantly at work defying his own natural laws at the petition and behest of suppliants who become unreasonably loaded with the expec-tation of 'having enough faith'. It is this last sting in the tail which can leave so many faithful intercessors and desperate implorers guiltily alienated from a God who appears to have let them down when their own particular solution to a prob-lem has not been activated.

On the other hand, it is easy to present a contour of God who is muzzled and reduced to the limited vulnerability of striving to enact his kingdom against all the odds, using only the limited natural processes open to him. The testimony of many faithful people over the centuries would affirm the reality of a God who is constantly and dynamically at work in his world.

Second-Isaiah speaks in paradoxical terms about the voca-tion of the individual and the nation. He believes passion-ately in a God who will act. Some of that action will be through the natural political and economic events of the day. Some of the action must be seen in poetic and image-built forms. Isaiah's faith is a faith rooted in a real and powerful God.

How God will 'bare his holy arm', to use Second-Isaiah's terminology for a pro-active God, is one of the curious revelations which seems to be vouchsafed to those who pray and intercede and search for the living God in a complex and divided world. Jesus said that everything would be in parables. Many would say that everything is in paradox. Peering into the cloud that hides the contours of God, some levels of rationality have to be abandoned, while the search for the magical and paranormal tends to be an alley rich only in disappointment. Perhaps the old adage: 'When you start praying, coincidences start happening' has more than a mite of truth.

Once, I attended a theological conference in Holland and of an afternoon drove into Amsterdam to visit the pictures at the Rijksmuseum. I gave a lift to two eminent professors of divinity. It happened that there was a strike of public transport drivers and the roads were particularly congested. Some local Dutch had advised against the journey and counselled parking a long way out of the city and taking an extended walk. Swept along by the traffic, we arrived in the centre and I began to make my way back towards the suburbs, with eyes open for parking which appeared to be impossible. Somewhat fatuously and to my shame, I said to my learned companions: 'What we need is an interventionist God'. Astonishingly, we rounded a corner only to find a vacant parking lot!

When I came to leave a parish after thirteen years in which I had sought to encourage the ministry of healing, I gave thanks in a sermon for, among many other thanksgivings, healings given. As people lined up to say goodbye to me, again and again, there were those who were able to acknowledge with me, change and transformation. Not one of those 'healings' was exactly 'miraculous'. All were the result of a mixture of medical support, prayer, friendship, anointing, services of healing, the care of the community. The reality of change was both explicit and implicit.

Signs of the presence of God are often there, if only one has the eyes to see. They are so often the result of the natural being unbelievably coincidental. I buried in South London a dear and good woman who had been a children's nanny all her life. When she died, she was very old and very infirm, though her capacity for friendship had attracted a surprising number of people to the funeral. As her coffin was loaded on to the hearse, a young woman walked by with two young children dancing and prancing on either hand, full of enthusiasm and children's vitality. As the hearse rounded the corner, an old man on his bicycle stopped and stood to attention, lifting his hat in salutation. Such an act was common years ago but is very rare in these days.

At a time of very considerable change in my own life, I was travelling back from the funeral of someone who had died suddenly leaving much unresolved and painful agenda. My mind was full of the many loose ends and uncertainties which the funeral experience had exposed. As I drove across a flooded landscape, on three separate occasions, a rainbow filled the sky. The implicit assurance that God is within all the ups and downs, the chances and changes of our lives, became explicit in the reappearance of the second and third rainbows.

Dag Hammarskjöld left behind the story of his spiritual journey which was found among his papers after his unexplained death in an air crash in the chaos of the Congo in 1962 and which was published under the title *Markings*. This remarkable Swedish negotiator and diplomat who became Secretary General of the United Nations reveals the story of an inner life which was often darkened by depression, despair and the shadows of suicide. Despite this reality, so unexposed in life, his writings describe many encounters with God which are full of affirmation, hope and response. Tireless in his efforts for world peace and often thwarted by setback, failure and intransigence, he speaks again and again of a 'yes' to God. In his diary for Whitsunday 1961, he wrote: 'I don't know who – or what – put the question, I don't know when it was put. I don't even remember answering. But at some moment I did answer Yes to Someone – or Something – and from that hour I was certain that existence is meaningful and that, therefore, my life, in self-surrender, had a goal'.[6]

Second-Isaiah would have known only too well what he meant!

Chapter 14

The Grandeur of God:

Job's Last Struggle

(Job 38.1 — 42.6)

THE WHOLE of the book of Job is a poetic story in which the age-old problem of human-kind's relationship with the realities of human experience is investigated. It is much more than a struggle to find an answer to the reason for human suffering and disaster. It is a book about one man's relationship with God. It is a book about feelings. It is a book about search and inner wrestling, about questions and about pain.

The book is an example of the Wisdom literature of the Near and Middle east. In the early days of human civilisation, the perennial problem of joy and pain and their explanation were as alive as they are today. There was considerable cross-fertilisation of philosophy and insight around the settlements of the fertile crescent and beyond. Israelite thought tapped into the general ferment of ideas and intellectual investigation. In the Wisdom literature of Israel, some of the great themes of Israelite thought: the selected vocation of the people, the Law, the Messianic hope, are virtually absent. Wisdom literature, expressed especially in the books of Proverbs, Ecclesiastes, and some of the psalms, as well as the book of Job, is concerned with the human condition, and with a perception about how it feels to be 'every-man' in God's world.

It is probable that the reign of Solomon encouraged and developed a growth in philosophy and inquiry. Solomon's reign, for all its latter-day religious syncretism and signs of effete royal decline, became renowned for its 'wisdom', as personified by the parable story of Solomon's judgement on the two prostitutes and the dead baby.[1] Solomon was an internationalist and traveller. He was concerned for a wider vision in diplomatic relationships. In some ways he was out of his time and, for all his failures, he was a prototype of that vocation to be a light to lighten the gentiles which was to become Israel's lost opportunity.

Some hold that the book of Job comes from the Solomonic period. Others hold that it is much later, post-exilic, perhaps about the year 400 BC. There is some comparable poetry that parallels the thought of Second-Isaiah. It is possible that the latter used Job's model of sacrificial suffering as he developed his own thought as expressed in the concept of the suffering servant. The setting of the book is in the patriarchal age. Job is not an Israelite but an Edomite sheikh and he lives not in the promised land flowing with milk and honey but on the fringes of the Edomite desert.

His situation is the situation of many. He has prospered. His life is full of good things. His relationships are good. He is respected. He is content. Into that situation of benevolent contentment comes a series of calamities which transform his life in a very short space of time into one of complete personal disaster, losing his wealth, his family and his health. Like so many in human experience, he struggles to make sense of his predicament and to understand the reason for the overthrow of his stability in what appears to be such a random and inexplicable way.

Much of the book is concerned with the personal struggle of Job under the influence of his three 'comforters' Eliphaz, Bildad and Zophar, to make religious and moral sense of his plight, and to plot the experience of his relationship with God which results. Indeed the quality of Job's capacity to trust God, good and God-fearing as he is alleged to be, is open to question from the outset. A Satan figure is presented in the courts of Heaven as implying that Job's faith is flawed by hypocrisy, that his trust is phoney and unreliable. Job is to be tested. Perhaps the roots of the old saying: 'These things are sent to try us' has its origin in the book of Job.

The book is a long and poetic story of encounter and struggle which concludes with the epic chapters when God 'answers Job out of the whirlwind'. In my early theological studies, I remember the lecturer, an Old Testament scholar of renown, remarking pithily that it would seem that the answer to the problem of suffering appears to be to visit a zoo and look, long and hard, at the crocodile! [2]

Job's encounter with God from which he makes a contour that leads him to repent and accept, comes in the last chapters when with graphic and imaginative beauty, the author describes something of the wonder of creation, the intricacy of its inter-related systems, the complexity of natural phenomena and the cohesive mystery of animal and bird life.

There is much in human experience that wrestles despairingly with human adversity which can seem to come, so often, in multiples. 'These things always come in threes.' 'I do not know what I did to deserve all this. I must have done something very wicked in my time.' 'I don't think I can take much more. How much more can a human being be supposed to take?' Doctors, social workers, clergy and all who live alongside people, come again and again upon situations of unbelievable random tragedy: one thing after another. Suffering is inexplicably indiscriminatory and seems to have its own way of re-visiting the heavy-laden. There can sometimes appear to be a bias towards invasion, once a defence has been breached. Tragedy can seem to follow itself. History carries this story. The plaques and memorials in churches and cathedrals tell again and again of multiple tragedy, of losses compounded, of misery long since buried but profound in the telling.

It is hardly surprising that this evidential experience either in oneself or the lives of others can lead to a belief in personal responsibility for what has befallen. The subtle insinuation for Job was simply that he had never trusted God sufficiently faithfully.

If this reaction is deep in human psychology, what sort of contour does it then make of God, indeed the 'God and Father of Our Lord Jesus Christ'? Lost becomes the incarnational faith of the God who emptied himself to lie in the helpless vulnerability of a Bethlehem stable, or to be a victim of the cruelty and intransigence of the hill they called the Skull. In its place is launched the God who tries us and tests us; the God who chooses the faithful for special treatments of endurance. Here is a God to be feared and placated for might he not choose one as God-fearing Job was chosen, just to see how one will handle the assault?

In practice, there is much of this kind of God in the book of Job, and so it must be seen in the context of the struggle for perception and the exposure of feelings under the attack of serious personal disaster. The conclusions in chapters 38–42 are not the conclusions of the New Testament, of a God who comes within the very struggle of human suffering to share, heal and redeem it. Job's God has other truths to disclose.

At the heart of Job's reconciliation within himself at what has happened to him, and within his understanding of God's part in what has befallen him, is a sense of the grandeur of God. Certainly God relates to Job. As Moses talks to God as a friend, so Job engages in long and disputatious dialogue with the Divine. At the end of the inner and the outer struggle, and despite the persuasions and delusions of the comforters, Job makes a contour of God which is shot through with a sense of awe at the magnificence of the whole created world and the complicated inter-relationship between biological and topographical systems. What Job finds all about him is so awe-inspiring and so full of wonder that he begins to see a perspective about his own struggles which find some kind of harmony in the on-goingness of the natural order.

It is one of the tragedies of modern industrial and urban society that it divorces people from contact with the complexity and grandeur of the natural world. Man has a deep need to relate to animals, and to find space for the apprehension of natural things. Children, again and again, are fulfilled by the possession of a pet. Hamsters, gerbils, guinea pigs, dogs, cats, fish all become cherished companions in life. A child bruised by suffering will turn to a pet for comfort and solace. How often has a dear dog, or cat, or some other special pet friend not been a life-saver in a crisis!

There is a loss in so many people's lives of the natural harmony with the living world. Pressure on space leads to overcrowded and man-made conditions. The grandeur of God's creative capacity can become lost, despite household animals, gardens and parks. The search for God ought to involve particular visits and holidays to places of space and natural beauty. Job began to make sense of his misfortune when he started to wonder at the feathers on a bird, at the cragginess of rocks, at the force of winds.

Laurens van der Post's studies of the Stone Age peoples of the Kalahari Desert reveal a deep harmony with, and natural love for, the world around. He describes in *The Heart of the Hunter* the wonder of a young mother lifting her infant child to the setting sun just to steep it in the beauty of 'its life-giving ray' in the words of the Celtic poetry of St Patrick's breastplate.[3] 'Slowly, against the water-light of the stars lapping briskly among the breakers of thorn and hardwood around us, emerged the outline of a woman holding out a child in both her hands, high above her head, and singing something with her own face lifted to the sky. Her attitude and the reverence trembling in her voice, moved me so that the hair at the back of my neck stood on end'.[4]

He describes too, in *A Mantis Carol* the community's thanksgiving in the fire-dance for life itself, and the reverence accorded to a gazelle which had been hunted and cooked. The book describes the memory of Hans Taaibosch, a bushman who had found his way to America, and who kept alive the tradition of his tribal roots. From those roots, the author reflects on his own experience of a bushman's dancing. 'He would dance out his gratitude to the animal his hunter had brought home for having been so good to allow itself to be killed so that he could continue to live .... All of desert nature was drawn in ... In the end the dancing produced such an atmosphere of oneness and belonging between all ... an act of natural communion with one of the greatest congregations of life ever gathered.'[5]

In Western society, wildlife parks sprang up in the boom days of the 70s and 80s as a way of responding to man's need to see and touch and be in tune with the animal kingdom. The popularity of a wildlife park reflects the human need for the kind of experience which Job so valued as he sought answers to the injustice of his condition.

Some friends of mine decided to take early retirement and to buy a croft in the North East of Scotland, and there to husband sheep, goats, highland cattle and to grow crops. Assisted certainly by retirement pensions, the smallholding became viable. Surrounded by sufficient space, they found welcome, encouragement and support from neighbouring farmers and crofters, although the life had a tough side. They discovered an inter-relatedness of human fellowship and joy in the care of animals living and being. It was nothing for a neighbour, a retired shepherd, to be up in the middle of the night to help with a ewe in a difficult labour. One spring evening, walking the goats up to the brow of a nearby hill and sitting with them while they grazed contentedly, with the Scottish hills all round, I was told that it had seemed like a glimpse of heaven.

Of course, the possibility of experiencing such a story is open only to a few, and there is much that is vicious and predatory about the natural world, and animal and bird life, but there is as well, in part, something about the grandeur and inter-relatedness which speaks of the contours of God.

I was told by a traveller returning from India, where he had visited a Christian convent, a derivative of the Oxford Mission, of the view of the Mother Superior. She had spoken of the difficulties of the Indianisation of a monastic concept whose roots lay in West European culture, but that all remained peaceful and constructive in the community just so long as all the sisters were handling and caring for animals.

There is much in us that wants to make God responsible for what happens to us. Human beings need authority and can recognise that the quality of a community is so often moulded by its head or leader. A school reflects the quality of the headteacher, a parish its minister, a company its managing director, a nation its president. We believe that God presents himself to us as 'The Boss', so that when our lives, as members of a community, become shot to pieces by disorder and tragedy, we can hold God to blame. Suffering must have been inflicted for a reason. If God is good, then the reason must be cathartic. It will do us good in the long run. The benevolent headmaster of a pre-war prep school brandishes his cane as the miscreant bends over for a thrashing and graciously declares: 'It hurts me more than it hurts you'.

Job can find no real answer for his suffering but there is a holiness about his determination that God is *not* to blame, and part of his inner struggle is to avoid the temptation to curse God for it all. What leads him to some kind of acceptance and personal harmony is a perception of the perspective of his own place in a complex and inter-related universe of which he is a member but not a controller.

Insights are beginning to abound about the complex and random way in which this planet and the universe of which it is only a minute part, has emerged. It would seem that laws of chance and necessity, of the anthropic principle, and quantum theory are suggesting that the existence of every one of us has much more to do with the spectacular emergence of life, out of a wealth of unlikely possibilities, than to the implementation of a Divine Master Plan. It came to be, but against all odds. My existence is more likely to be the result of an incredibly intricate web of genetic and emotional possibilities, ending in the emergence of me, than in some deliberate act of creation by a purpose-bent God. Purpose there undoubtedly is, but the purpose is enshrined in the emergence of creative strength out of all sorts of possible options.

I once had a vision of a bizarre experiment. This involved taking to the top of the tower of my large parish church, two tons of mixed bridal confetti. From the top, all the confetti was poured to the ground, aided by a gusting wind. The number of combinations in which the pattern of the confetti might fall must have been in trillions. It occurred to me, as I pondered this, that if each combination represented a human life, in each would God work and fashion and create. With each changing pattern, as the breeze disturbed the mould of each of the trillions of designs, would God work creatively and dynamically. Here, it seemed to me, was something of the grandeur of God who is within all that befalls the evolutionary process of his emerging world. 'Where were you when I laid the foundations of the earth? Do you know when the mountain goats bring forth? Do you observe the calving of the hinds?' asks God of Job.[5]

The Wisdom literature for all its imaginative efforts to search for understanding had none of the insights available to us. Creation would have seemed to be a one-off act from which God stood back, and controlled. Perhaps some of that more primitive perception lingers on all too rootedly in the hearts of the modern faithful. He who is in that sort of control must surely be responsible for the mis-control of my life, when it leads into the disasters of personal and financial ruin, the collapse of health, and the death of those I love.

Job discovered a new perspective in reflecting his comparative insignificance as it related to the complex divine ordering of the natural world. For our generation, in its post-Newtonian understandings of the astonishing warp and weave of intricate eco-systems and complicated molecular structures, the grandeur of God may come in another way.

A contour of God which is common both to the desert poet and to the modern caller upon God is a sense of God's greatness and splendour and grandeur. In the heart of bitter and disillusioning suffering, it is easy to fantasise about some kind of Master Controller who, either because 'He knows best' or, and this is more sinister, because it is somehow 'for our good', makes us endure. In times of real desperation such a God may even seem like a divine torturer against whom we rail like the unrepentant thief on the cross.

A more authentic contour is the God who is deeply involved, both near and far, in a whole realm of creative possibilities. In such a world, as has evolved through the initiation of the creative process and through the emergence of laws of dependence and chance, such a God is deeply involved. In the web of possibilities that is the life of every individual, all sorts of chances may emerge, both positive and negative. It is possible both to win the jackpot in the National Lottery and to crash my car on the M1 in fog killing my wife and children. Both eventualities are unlikely but possible. If either occurs, I will surely need the sustaining power of God to use creatively the results of both experiences. As the confetti blows down from the church tower, it is unlikely, but possible, that I will be able to predict how a particular pattern will fall. The awesome grandeur, which is God, is perceivable both in the mystery of the natural world in all its overt splendour, from mountain goats to the pattern of clouds; and in the intricacies of the variable chances and changes of a human life. For Job, God was both near and far, both approachable and distant. Our own perceptions are likely to be no different. We would be wise to hold on to his grandeur, which may manifest itself unexpectedly and wondrously as much either in the majesty of our experience of great natural beauty, as in the simple faithfulness in the eyes of an old woman about to die.

Job's encounter with God offers no explanation for the existence of suffering either generically or in his own life. The problem of pain and undeserved misery remains insoluble in rational terms. There is no explanation, only the reality. It is the New Testament which offers a window into God's involvement in the suffering of Job. The cross stands as our paradigm of hope and of our evidence of God's activity and response.

In the encounter at the end of the book, Job glimpses something of the proportion of man to God and in the delineation of that proportion, he sees the grandeur of God. Paradoxically, that grandeur is not isolating and distancing but curiously bridge-building, perhaps simply because the questions are asked directly: 'Where were *you* ...?'

There is much in the contour of God that is enfolding and overshadowing. There is much again that is extending and unknowing. At the heart of the Christian Gospel is not only the cross of suffering, which is human-kind's answer to the love of its initiator, but also the Resurrection which is again and again the creative evidence of the divine will to rebuild and restore God's world.

The suffering of Job is its own paradigm of the suffering of countless million victimised, abused, disordered, disaster-struck lives. Job is representative of it all. What he teaches is that his misfortune is not the fault of God. Such a perspective is for Job simply too narrow. The shape and contour of God for him is simply too awesomely, wonderfully, extensively dynamic and creative to be trivialised to the level of being the author of his tribulation.

There are many, many people over the Christian centuries who, through tragedies of desperate proportions, have glimpsed the reality of God's presence and creative will to use the very stuff of suffering as the seed-corn for renewal and change. The first glimpse of that evidence was to be seen through the tear-glazed eyes of those early visitors to a burial garden in the mists of the dawn of a Palestinian day. When the author of St John's gospel sought to record, with such intricate perception, the whole revelation of God's being in the 'Word become flesh, full of grace and truth',[7] and so full of grace and truth as to be also: 'The Resurrection and the Life',[8] he enshrined his own words of insight in the mouth of Christ in St John 5.17. There are many ways of translating the Greek text but it could be that for Job the ring of truth would have been: 'My father has never yet finished his work and I am working too'.[9]

Chapter 15

The God of Blessing and Provision:

Abraham Prepares to Sacrifice his Son

(Genesis 22. 1–19)

THERE IS a sense in which many spiritual journeys end where they began. In a way, that is hardly surprising if God is in all and over all; if he is both faithful in his constancy and dynamic in his activity. Old Testament revelations teach us not only something about our spiritual roots but also offer their own glimpses into the varying shapes of God which encounters with him describe. This book began with the call of Abraham, which gives its own insight into the beckoning nature of God's persistent call into risk-taking and adventure. It ends with that unnatural encounter described in Genesis chapter 22, when Abraham's will to respond to the call of God, whatever the cost, appears to have reached scales of fanatical fidelity: the old man is prepared to offer his precious son as a sacrifice to the God whom he trusts, in line with the practices of child sacrifice already well known in primitive Canaanite folklore.

The story, as presented, is frighteningly threatening. What kind of God could demand the will to sacrifice something as precious as an only son to prove that commitment to his inscrutable ways was that secure in its bonding? There is something uncomfortable about the use of the story in the liturgy for Good Friday as a way of introducing insight into the mystery of the atonement. It presents an image of propitiation and substitution which clouds the insights into the vulnerability and suffering of God which the crucifixion also so clearly reveals. Indeed sacrificial theology has rooted itself in the Christian tradition to the point where, in some areas, it may positively hinder perceptions about the all-inclusiveness and outstanding love and individual concern of God, which these chapters have tried to reveal.

There may be a sense in which the story identifies with something in us that feels in a shadowy way that perhaps, after all, God really is like the kind of God who demands the ultimate from us and that, even then, that will not be enough. Religious persuasion can reveal its own dark side, and the stories of an abounding variety of cults and their methods reveal only too tragically how the potential liberation of faith can become subverted into a tragic form of spiritual slavery. Mainstream Churches will all know examples of religious persuasion which appear to be anything but liberation. There is a fanatical side to many manifestations of religious commitment and the life and history of the Church has been far from immune from dogmatic delusion. Has the story anything to teach us about the contours of God as we might perceive him today, or is it simply a parody figment of early man's religious consciousness?

In the story of Abraham, the event takes place at the conclusion of his life. Family and neighbour reconciliation has effectively been achieved. The future is assured. In the patriarchal tradition, the story of a covenant relationship with the one true God has begun. This is the end of the beginning. This story of Abraham's near-sacrifice of Isaac is the crowning conclusion to the prologue which preludes the long story of the evolution of religious faith between God and his people. Indeed there is a crucial decisiveness about Abraham's faith. Because he is prepared to go this far, because nothing, even the preciousness of the beloved and only son of his old age, is to be allowed to stand in the way of his trust in God, so he will indeed be blessed and be a blessing to others.

Isaac, unwitting of the appalling plans of his father, and seeing the fire and the wood, asks where is the lamb for the burnt offering. The reply is: 'God will provide himself the lamb for the burnt offering, my son'.[1] From this statement develops, in due course, a whole range of thought which sees Jesus as the lamb of God who will be the sacrifice provided by God. It could be that much Christian thought, as it becomes focused on the person of Jesus in the drama of the crucifixion, pulls into its corporate subconscious an image of the kind of God who provides himself with a sacrifice, and, with an even more sinister undertone, needs one. While at an overt level, this may be a way of describing the ultimacy of God's love, who in the words of St John 'so loved the world that he gave his only son',[2] it may carry with it a variety of mixed perceptions about the way in which Jesus propitiates the father, and leaves all sorts of unanswered questions about how God could allow the reality of the sacrifice. It is the approval rating that Abraham wins for his willingness to sacrifice Isaac that may introduce some obscurely bewildering perceptions about God, as we try to relate to the cross, even seen through the light of the resurrection, but the theology of the cross is outside the scope of this book.

Where are the contours of God in the story of the willingness of Abraham to sacrifice his son Isaac, and what sort of encounter could it have been that led Abraham to obey the command, and then to be released from the obligation at the eleventh hour?

It is of course possible that Abraham simply misunderstood the original command, but in the text the instructions are clear enough. Somewhere in the passing down of the oral tradition amongst the tribesmen round the desert campfires, the terrifying demand of God was enshrined.

In searching for contours of the living God which are alive and healing and real and restorative, we may need to be ever mindful of the fact that we may have missed the message or simply muddled thoroughly the divine initiative. It is a dangerous premise to be too adamant about the hard-and-fastness of an encounter. God is weaving his own pattern with our lives as we obey, disobey, misread and re-read. The need for alertness, discernment and interpretation is a prerequisite for our spiritual journeys.

According to the story, Abraham does not appear to have made a mistake. He has become convinced that the sacrifice is what God requires. So the story tells us first that there is in the contour of God a requirement which asks of us to be ready to give up, to the extent of costly sacrifice, and that that giving up is an ingredient which unleashes resource and power. It is an important facet to hold in mind. Christian communities are made up of a few who are sacrificing far too much of their time, their energy and their resource, while a much larger majority lives on the fat of that giving and fool themselves into believing that they have given much when they have given very little.

Sacrifice has a God-like redemptive quality about it, and there are many people who have given something of themselves in so very many different ways and found in the giving a costly but generous reward.

To know God is to be prepared to give him something of one self. Abraham and Isaac, father and son, are deeply identified in each other, because Isaac is the precious heir. It is Abraham's willingness to give the wholeness of himself which is the entry point into a future with God. Representing, as Abraham does, the beginning of human-kind's faith story, his willingness to give of himself to the God who has become the heart of his life, stands as a point of discovery for all people who seek to find God. It is in the step forward, with the most precious in one's hand, that the window on to God can become opened and the raindrops of blessing pour down.

Because of Abraham's obedience, a divine promise seems to be enabled and which thus becomes indelibly part of the spiritual contract. Obedience will lead to both personal blessing, and the gift of being a blessing to others. The story could be said to have a parable symbolism. In terms of the faith story of the Judao-Christian tradition, this is the initiative which is the parallel to the 'big bang' in the evolution of matter and thus, eventually, of this planet as we know it.

It is at the beginning of his spiritual journey that Abraham takes the risk of an uncertain adventure into the future and so begins the story of the disclosure of the God who is. It is at the end of his life that his risk-taking qualities are put under another terrifying scrutiny and again he is not found wanting. So from the pages of these ancient roots, we learn something about God that will never change: the more we give, the more we receive; the more we can offer him, the more he can use us for his glory; the more deeply we can hand over the gifts and talents with which he has endowed us, the more those gifts and talents will be used for the blessing and healing of the world.

Such a comforting and immensely enriching certainty of God's nature has its counter-side. Often we have to hold on through all sorts of periods of bewilderment and misdirection waiting patiently in the darkness for the certainty of the dawn. We can never know what passed through Abraham's mind as he cast off from his young men and the donkey and set forth with his son, the wood, and the fire and the knife. There is something in us that can admire the resolution if there is much that deplores the folly. Perhaps his very determination forms its own signpost of warning. Seen from a Christian perspective, in those early patriarchal days, the Holy Spirit had not yet been given, and the Johannine promise is that through the Spirit we shall be led into all truth. The story itself is a lesson about asking questions and making one's search and exploring divine territory, lest we be those who set forth to worship, but with a knife in our hands, and so have misread the contours of the living God.

What we do know from the story is that delivery was given and given just in time. Abraham's second command from God was to withhold himself from the dreadful sacrifice, for he had proved his faithfulness.

Perhaps there are two stars of truth held in tandem in the night sky of the story, to illuminate the reality of the contour and shape of God known to all who call upon his name. One star might suggest that although the story appears to be about the faithfulness of Abraham, it is really a story about the faithfulness of God. The image has become juxtaposed from the root, like some ancient tree in which the trunk and stem have entwined themselves in a gnarled convolution of upward thrust. Because Abraham has been faithful, he will be both blessed and a blessing; and the expression of that blessedness and blessing will be nothing less than the faithfulness of God to be God in whatever contour or shape he discloses himself to us, in the myriad twists and turnings of our varying encounters with him.

The second star is simply this: Once the dreadful moment has passed and Isaac is to be spared, Abraham looks and behold there is a ram caught in a thicket. 'So Abraham called the name of that place "The Lord will provide".' [3]

As every person of faith weaves their particular route through the chances and changes of life, discovering and rediscovering again the nature and contour of the God who is at the heart of all, there is a promise of provision which is never failing and ever resourceful. Whatever the particular struggle, however pinned down inch by inch on the climb up the north face of the Eiger, or desperately traumatised by one's own personal Calvary, or however one may express the particular struggles and desolations of life, it is at the heart of faithful experience that the Lord does indeed provide, often in the most unexpected and surprising ways. In the dark days of the first year of the Second World War, King George VI chose to quote the words of Minnie Louise Haskins, in his Christmas broadcast:

> 'I said to the man who stood at the gate of the year: "Give me a light that I may tread safely into the unknown". And he replied: "Go out into the darkness and put your hand into the hand of God. That shall be to you better than light and safer than a known way!" So I went forth and finding the hand of God, trod gladly into the night. And He led me towards the hills and the breaking of day in the lone East'. [4]

The writer of the letter to the Hebrews declares: 'For here we have no lasting city, but we seek the city which is to come!' [5] Meister Eckhart, the German medieval mystic puts it another way: 'There is no stopping place in this life. No, nor was there ever one for anyone, no matter how far along the way they have come. This then, above all things, be ready for the gifts of God and for new ones.' [6]

It was ever thus!

NOTES

Introduction

1. *The Song of the Bird* by Anthony de Mello, Image Books: 1984. p3. Doubleday Publishing: New York: First published September 1984.

2. *The Dart of Longing Love*, edited Robert Llewelyn: 1983. p5. Darton, Longman and Todd.

3. *A Lesson of Love: The Revelations of Julian of Norwich*, edited Father John-Julien OJN: 1988. p11. Darton, Longman and Todd.

Chapter 1

1. Genesis: 15.1

2. Luke: 5.4

3. *The Divine Risk*, edited by Richard Holloway: 1990. Darton, Longman and Todd. p38.

4. Mark: 1.17–18

Chapter 2

1. Genesis: 30

2. Quoted in: *C.S. Lewis, a biography*, by A.N. Wilson. Harper Collins Publishers Limited. 1990. p207.

3. Genesis: 28.16

4. Genesis: 28.17

5. *English Hymnal*: Hymn 444 written by Sarah Adams 1805–48. Oxford University Press, first published 1906.

6. Luke: 17.20–21

Chapter 3

1. Exodus: 3.3

2. *The Wind in the Willows* by Kenneth Grahame. Methuen, first published 1908.

3. Exodus: 3.11

4. Matthew: 10.29, 31

Chapter 4

1. Luke: 1.34

2. Psalm: 27.6

3. *A Lesson of Love: Julian of Norwich*. Ibid. p144.

4. Exodus: 33.14

5. The Wreck of the Deutschland, by G.M. Hopkins, from *Poems of Gerard Manley Hopkins*. 3rd edition: Oxford University Press. 1948. p67.

6. Psalm: 18.12
7. Matthew: 28.20

Chapter 5

1. *A Lesson of Love: Julian of Norwich*. Ibid. p69
2. Mark: 8.35
3. Joshua: 1.5
4. Psalm: 18.18
5. Joshua: 1.5
6. Psalm: 4.1
7. Joshua: 1.5
8. Joshua: 1.9
9. John: 3.14–15
10. John: 12.32

Chapter 6

1. 1 Samuel: 3.1
2. Quoted in: *Jesus Ahead*, by Gerard Bessiere. Burns and Oates. 1975. p49.
3. 1 Samuel: 2.8
4. *A Lesson of Love: Julian of Norwich*. Ibid. p213.
5. Ibid. p125.
6. Ibid. p117.
7. *The Lion, the Witch and the Wardrobe*, by C.S. Lewis. Lions, Collins Publishing Group, first published 1950. p148.
8. 1 Samuel: 3.19
9. Luke: 10.21

Chapter 7

1. 1 Samuel: 8.6 & 22
2. Ibid. 10.22
3. Ibid. 10.6
4. Ibid. 9.2
5. Ibid. 17.5–6
6. Ibid. 16.13–14
7. Ibid. 15.9–23
8. Ibid. 17.42 (NEB)
9. Ibid. 17.40
10. Ibid. 17.47
11. 1 Corinthians: 1.26 & 27

12. Luke: 12.32
12. *The Life and Death of Dietrich Bonhoeffer*, by Mary Bosanquet, Hodder and Stoughton, 1968. pp229 & 233.
13. The 20th of July by H.H. Kirst, English Translation published by William Collins Sons & Co. Ltd, 1966. p111. Harper Collins Publishers Limited.
14. 1 Samuel: 17.47
15. Acts: 1.6–8

Chapter 8

1. 1 Kings: 9.1–9
2. 1 Kings: 3.5
3. *Meditations on the Sand*, by Alessandro Pronzato, St Paul Publications: 1982. p60.
4. Ibid. p35
5. *The Prophet*, by Kahlil Gibran, William Heinemann Ltd, first published 1926. pp81 & 82.
6. *1662 Book of Common Prayer.*
7. Mark: 4.24–25
8. B.C.P. Ibid.

Chapter 9

1. 1 Kings: 19.4
2. 1 Kings: 19.9
3. *The Lake Isle of Innisfree*, by William Butler Yeats, Oxford Book of English Verse: 1925. No. 864. p1039.
4. Psalm: 139.6–9
5. 1 Kings: 19.10
6. 1 Kings: 19.14
7. *School for Prayer* by Metropolitan Anthony Bloom. Libra Books, Darton Longman and Todd, 1970. pp60–61.
8. The Prophet, Ibid. p71.
9. *A Lesson of Love: Julian of Norwich.* Ibid. pp74 & 75.
10. Mark: 6.31–32.

Chapter 10

1. Isaiah: 6.1
2. Psalm: 18.8
3. *Four Quartets*, by T.S. Eliot, Faber and Faber, Ltd., 1944. p36.
4. *Selected Poems*, by T.S. Eliot, Faber and Faber, Ltd., 1954. pp97 & 98.

5. *The Shape of the Liturgy,* by Dom Gregory Dix, Dacre Press, Westminster. p744.

6. 2 Corinthians: 5.17

7. Isaiah: 6.8

Chapter 11

1. *Brewer's Dictionary of Phrase and Fable* Cassell plc. 1959. p585.

2. Jeremiah: 1.5

3. Ibid. 1.6

4. Ibid. 1.10

5. *The Alternative Services Book 1980.* © Central Board of Finance of the Church of England. p358.

6. Jeremiah: 1.5

7. Romans: 8.30

8. Jeremiah: 32.15

9. *A Lesson of Love: Julian of Norwich.* Ibid. p67.

10. *St Augustine: Confessions.*

11. Acts: 9.15

12. *The Prophet,* Ibid. p110.

Chapter 12

1. Ezekiel: 8

2. Ezekiel: 1.2

3. John: 10.14

4. Matthew: 9.36

5. Four Quartets, by T.S. Eliot Ibid. pp42 & 43.

6. Luke: 19.41

7. Ibid. 13.34

8. *A Lesson of Love; Julian of Norwich.* Ibid. p155.

9. Ibid.

10. *Grey is the Colour of Hope,* by Irina Ratushinskaya, Hodder and Stoughton Ltd/New English Library Ltd. First printed 1988. pp117, 283.

11. Ibid. p283.

12. *Jesus, Son of Man,* by Kahlil Gibran, William Heinemann Ltd, first published 1928. p197.

13. Mark: 6.37. Luke: 9.13

14. St Teresa of Avila (1515–82) Prayer and her Bookmark.

15. Mark: 4.24

16. *Home-thoughts from Abroad*, by Robert Browning. Oxford Book of English Verse, Ibid. No 729. p866.
17. Ezekiel 34.13 & 14
18. ASB Ibid. p356.
19. Ezekiel: 34.11 & 12

Chapter 13

1. Isaiah: 49.3
2. *Devotions upon emergent occasions*, by John Donne Concise Dictionary of Religious Quotations, A.R. Mowbray. 1975. No.6. p36.
3. Isaiah: 49.4
4. Ibid. v.6
5. Ibid. v.5
6. *Markings* by Dag Hammarskjold. (Translated by W.H. Auden & Leif Sjoberg). Faber and Faber Ltd. 1964. p 169.

Chapter 14

1. 1 Kings: 3.16–28
2. Job: 40.15–41.34
3. *New English Hynmal*: No.159, St Patrick's Breastplate, Translated by Mrs C.F. Alexander, 1818–95. The Canterbury Press, Norwich.
4. *The Heart of the Hunter*, by Laurens van der Post, Penguin Books Ltd. First published by The Hogarth Press Ltd, 1961. pp42 & 43.
5. *A Mantis Carol*, by Laurens van der Post, Hogarth Press Ltd. 1975. pp110 & 111.
6. Job: 3. 4–39.1
7. John: 1.14
8. Ibid. 11.25
9. Ibid. 5.17

Chapter 15

1. Genesis: 22.8
2. John: 3.16
3. Genesis: 22.14
4. Minnie Louise Haskins (1875–1957) from: *The Desert*, poem privately printed 1908.
5. Hebrews: 13.14
6. Meister Eckhart. (1260–1327).

ACKNOWLEDGEMENTS

The author is grateful to the following copyright owners and publishers for permission to reproduce extracts from their works: A. & C. Black (Publishers) Ltd, *The Shape of the Liturgy* by Dom Gregory Dix; Burns and Oates Ltd, *Jesus Ahead* by Gerard Bessiere; Cassell plc, *Brewer's Dictionary of Phrase and Fable* (Cassell & Co. 1959), and *Concise Dictionary of Religious Quotations* (A. R. Mowbray 1975); Darton, Longman and Todd, *School for Prayer* Metropolitan Anthony Bloom (1970), *The Dart of Longing Love* by Robert Llewelyn (1983), *A Lesson of Love* Edited and translated by Father John Julian, OJN (1988), *The Divine Risk* Edited by Richard Holloway (1990); Doubleday, *The Song of the Bird* by Anthony de Mello; Faber and Faber Ltd, *Four Quartets* 1944 and *Selected Poems* 1954 by T. S. Eliot, and *Markings* by Dag Hammarskjold translated by W. H,. Auden and Leif Sjoberg; Harper Collins Publishers Limited, *The Psalms the New Translation* by Frost, Emerton and Macintosh, *C. S. Lewis: A Biography* by A. N. Wilson, *The Lion, the Witch and the Wardrobe* by C. S. Lewis (Lions 1980, an imprint of the Children's Division of Harper Collins Publishers Limited, *The 20th of July*, by H. H. Kirst (English translation by William Collins Sons & Co. Ltd 1966); Hodder and Stoughton Publishers, *Grey is the colour of hope* by Irena Ratushinksaya (New English Library Ltd, Permission No. CF/B 0994. © Seahorse Inc. 1988); Laurence Pollinger and Estate of Mary Bosanquet, *The Life and Death of Dietrich Bonhoeffer;* Chatto & Windus (Random House), *The Heart of the Hunter* and *A Mantis Carol* both by Laurens van der Post; St Paul Publications, *Meditations on the Sand* 1982 by Alessandro Pronzato.

All scripture quotations are from *The Revised Standard Version of the Bible*. Copyright: 1946, 1952, 1971 by the Division of Christian Education of the National Council of Churches of Christ in the U.S.A. except in one instance from the *New English Bible*: Oxford University Press. Cambridge University Press.

Extracts from The Book of Common Prayer, the rights in which are vested in the Crown, are reproduced by permission of the Crown's Patentee, Cambridge University Press.

Extracts from The Alternative Service Book 1980, which is copyright © the Central Board of Finance of the Church of England, are used with permission.

Index

137